CULTURAL SERVICES

Cultural Services Headquarters,
Red Doles Lane,
Huddersfield. West Yorks. HD2 1YF

LIBERTY OR DEATH
Radicals, Republicans and Luddites
c. 1793-1823

Yet, Freedom! yet thy banner,
Torn, but flying
Streams like a thunderstorm,
Against the wind.

G.Byron
Childe Harold's Pilgrimage
xcviii

Alan Brooke & Lesley Kipling
© 1993.

Printed by Garian Press, Unit 10, The Gatehouse Centre,
Albert St, Lockwood, Huddersfield. HD1 3QD
(Tel: 0484 435498)

Published by
Workers History Publications
59, Magdale, Honley

This is the fifth in a series of booklets intended to raise awareness of local
working class history.
A list of other publications is available from the publisher.

Acknowledgements

The authors wish to thank the staff of West Yorkshire Archive Service
at Calderdale, Kirklees and Leeds for their help in using documents
and permission to quote therefrom. The Keeper of the Public Records
for permission to use Crown Copyright Home Office papers.
Olive, Countess Fitzwilliam's Wentworth Settlement Trustees and the
Director, Sheffield City Libraries, for permission to quote from
the Wentworth Woodhouse Muniments.
We would also like to thank John Rumsby, Senior Officer (Museums),
Kirklees Cultural Services, for advice on aspects of military
history and for permission to use the Skelmanthorpe flag illustration;
Stephen Whitwam, Huddersfield Family History Society, for
help with the Mellor family tree and other genealogical queries; and
Dr Lance Tufnell, for metereological information.
Also we are indebted to Victoria Minton for logistical support and
proof reading. The authors take full responsibility for any errors
or opinions in the final work.

Cover: Illustration from the revolutionary street fighting manual
Defensive Instructions for the People
by Colonel Macerone, on sale in Huddersfield c.1833

ISBN 0 9522549 0 5

THE RIGHTS OF MAN

As the eighteenth century entered its final decade, the industrial revolution was as yet barely perceptible in Huddersfield and neighbouring parishes. A few small scribbling mills, and even fewer large factories, had been built on new sites in the valleys, whilst only a handful of chimneys betrayed the presence of steam engines. Enclosure had already divided the ancient uncultivated commons of some townships into neat fields, marking the advent of agricultural 'improvement'. But, over the next thirty years, industrial capitalism was to impose an unprecedented acceleration in the rate of economic and technological change. No less profound was the rapid transformation in the social and political landscape.

An aristocratic and commercial elite held a monopoly of political power which even excluded many of the growing class of capitalists. But a storm was gathering which was to shake the old order and open the stage to ordinary people. No longer would they be 'the mob' manipulated by this or that aristocratic faction, but citizens fighting for their own rights and liberties. The American colonists were the first to show that it was possible to establish a government of the people. The Irish middle classes under Henry Grattan, stirred by the example, asserted in arms the independence of a parliament representing their class. In Britain itself, a large section of the Whig party demanded the reform of a rotten parliament dominated by 'boroughmongers', the aristocracy and their minions, so that it would represent all men of property. There was growing political enthusiasm as 1788 marked the centenary of the 'Glorious Revolution' against James II - an unfinished revolution which had curbed some of the power of the monarchy, only to raise an oligarchy of landed aristocrats and commercial interests in its place. The following year it seemed that a new era had begun and Charles Fox, the champion of parliamentary reform, spoke for many when he hailed the French revolution as 'the greatest event that ever happened in the world! And how much the best!' [1]

But the French revolution was no exclusive gentlemanly affair as 1688 had been, nor was it carried through mainly by farmers, tradesmen and merchants as in America. It was a genuine popular revolution, with the peasants and *sans culottes*, the working people, as the driving force. As the enthusiasm of middle class supporters in Britain waned and Edmund Burke attacked those who encouraged the unrest of the 'swinish multitude,' it was left to Britain's *sans culottes*, the workers and artisans, to take up the cause. Their aspirations were articulated by a man whose life and work came to symbolise the American and French revolutions and who, in his rebuttal of Burke in the pages of the *Rights of Man,* laid the foundations of modern democratic thought.

Tom Paine asserted that rights were not bequeathed by virtue of a mythical constitution, but that each individual enjoyed natural rights and, by his place in society, civil rights. Present generations had no obligation to be ruled by the deeds of their ancestors, since 'governments arise either out of the people, or over the people.' The English government was of the latter kind, originally imposed on the English people by the Norman conquest and consolidated by a supine aristocracy in 1688. Government took two forms, monarchical, - hereditary and aristocratic - ; or republican - representative and democratic. The former led to wars and a heavy burden of taxes, and was on the way out. Now 'It is an age of Revolution in which everything may be looked for.' Revolutions 'are become subjects of universal conversation, and may be considered as the order of the day.' They would create a new Republican age of 'Government founded on a moral theory, on a system of universal peace, on the indefeasible hereditary Rights of Man.' A true Republican government would also have a welfare system to look after its poorer citizens. Paine did not expound a strategy for revolution. He intended that it should be achieved peaceably, but, as his support for the American revolution and the storming of the Bastille showed, he did not balk at armed struggle.

'Reason and discussion, persuasion and conviction, become the weapons of the contest, and it is only when those are attempted to be suppressed that recourse is had to violence.' [2]

This was a precept which was to guide Republicans over the following half century.

Membership Card of the United Britons c. 1802

SPIRIT OF PERSECUTION
Repression and the Rights of Man 1793-1795

The *Rights of Man,* published in two parts in early 1791 and 1792, ran into hundreds of thousands of copies, which, even opponents agreed, permeated almost every working class community in Britain. The Sheffield Society for Constitutional Information, founded by workers and artisans at the end of 1791, was the first organisation specifically created to promote the ideas of the *Rights of Man.* It was followed by the London Corresponding Society, which became the centre of a network of similar bodies in towns throughout the country.[1]

Opinion polarised further as France deposed its king and declared a Republic. After February 1793, when Britain joined the attempt of the European monarchs to destroy the revolutionary regime, sympathy for Paine's views became portrayed as support for an alien creed propagated by the country's enemies. The term *'Jacobin',* taken from what was seen as the most hard-line Republican faction in the French Convention, was applied by 'Church and King' loyalists to working class opponents of the government with the same vehemence, and little regard for accuracy, as 'Communist' was to be in the twentieth century. An anonymous loyalist leaflet published in Huddersfield in 1793, described the political ferment and warned against the spread of seditious ideas:

> **'In this time of general argument and debate, when the members of every workshop form a Privy Council and the village public house can boast its Parliament; when pamphlets are industriously dispersed amongst you containing plausible but false reasonings...'**

At least one group of men in the town were seriously discussing such dangerous literature and sent a plaintive appeal to the London Corresponding Society for more, 'for God's sake send us word of enlightenment and philanthropy. Huddersfield abounds in true patriots, but we are beset by masses of ignorant aristocracy.' 'Friends' from Huddersfield were among others from across the West Riding who gathered at Halifax in April 1794 to plan support for a 'National Convention' - interpreted by the authorities as part of a sinister plot to establish an alternative, revolutionary government. [2]

One of those involved in a Corresponding Society, or similar body, in Huddersfield, was George Dyson, a book-keeper and warehouseman for the manufacturer John Whitacre of Woodhouse Mill, Deighton. On 9 March he wrote to a fellow Baptist, Tom Stutterd, a commercial traveller for the firm, who was away on business. After a mundane complaint that the cloth dressers weren't helping out with packing pieces, he enquired whether down South,

'republicanism begins again to lift up her head? In our parts I believe
things are growing very serious. I wish we may have peace in the land but
I think we shall not long have, there has been an express from Edinburgh
at the different societies for parliamentary reform and from hints which he
dropped and from other things which we hear it is generally believed the
nation will rise up in arms in the same hour. I mean England and Scotland
and that period is not far off...'

Whether, at this time, there actually was a revolutionary organisation with
plans for an armed uprising, Dyson certainly thought so. 'A person told me
some matters lately which quite astonished me. I did not think the half was
going forward which is.' The man showed him a ticket depicting the figure of a
woman carrying a cap of liberty and trampling on chains over the motto *'Man
knows no Master save creating heaven or such as choice and common good
ordains.'* The fact that George was taken into confidence would indicate that he
was considered a reliable sympathiser at least, but still he felt that he was not
kept informed of everything, 'There is something of secrecy in the societies
going forward which very few of the members know of, save the principal or
leading men.' He had also heard that someone in the Huddersfield area had
refused a request to provide 50 stand of arms. In his letter he included the full
text of resolutions agreed at a Sheffield meeting on 28 February, condemning
the war and thanking Earl Stanhope for a speech in support of Muir and Palmer,
transported for organising a Convention in Scotland.

Arrests increased over the following months as the Habeas Corpus
Suspension Act in May introduced internment without trial. One of the
Huddersfield magistrates, R.H.Beaumont of Whitley Hall, ordered the arrest of
the 'Sheffield News' man, on 6 June. According to Dyson, 'they took him
somewhere about Honley, they handcuffed him and sent him to York Castle. I
don't know what his crime was but suppose it was for selling seditious
pamphlets.' The 'Sheffield News' is perhaps a reference to the *Sheffield
Register*, which at this time was forced to close when its editor Joseph Gales
was threatened with arrest. Dyson and sixteen others subscribed to the *English
Chronicle* instead. Dyson himself and a friend and workmate, Thomas B.,
came to the attention of Beaumont, who told their employer that they had been
to a Sheffield meeting and bought seditious material. Questioned by Whitacre,
Dyson replied that he had bought sermons by Joseph Priestley, an account of the
trial of the dissenting minister William Winterbottom, (subversive enough
works to some), and similar tracts - '...respecting the other small things which
we bought,' he wrote to Stutterd a few days later :

'I did not mention as I thought I had no right to be mine own accuser. I
really wish Mr W. would not harass my mind so much. I begin to be
almost disgusted at one thing and another. We are now at a horrible pass
in this country, people must not talk, nor read, nor write...perhaps I shall

**date my letter from the Bastile and if I do you may quake for fear on your
return home, our T.B. is also accused of preaching sedition, but he says he
knows nothing of the matter. I tell him Mr Winterbotham was the same
and he is in prison. I am very much out of humour respecting our affair...'**

He concluded with a cryptic PS,

**'What think you, is it wisdom for you to keep your papers at large? Law
there is none and if a search warrant is issued there will be no alternative
but to prison, innocence is of no avail. Mine I have destroyed.' 3**

Whitacre even regarded his journeyman clothdressers' signing of a
petition for parliamentary reform as an act of personal disloyalty, demanding at
least their neutrality, 'If they would not have acted with me, they should not
have acted against me.' George took the easy way out, signing neither the
petition or the loyal Address supported by Whitacre. 'I suppose we may be
termed cowards,' he reflected, 'but quietness in a person's own family is a
blessing.' Whitacre reinforced his message to his servants by plastering his mill
and cloth-dressing shop with posters commanding *'Fear God and Honour the
King'* and *'Study to be quiet and mind your own business.'* Despite such
intimidation from employers, 'especially Messrs Horsfall', over 2,000 names
were collected.

Beaumont's efforts to root out Jacobinism almost sparked a spy-scare in
the town. Two Frenchmen, Barbiere and de Larche, representatives of the
National Assembly, had arrived in Huddersfield in 1792 to buy cloth for the
French Army. They were said to be outspoken Republicans in favour of a
revolution in Britain. Strangely though, they not only remained after the
outbreak of war, but resided at the house of the prosperous mill owner and
merchant, Law Atkinson, leading Loyalist and an officer in Huddersfield
Volunteer Corps, set up in case of an invasion by the French or an uprising by
home-grown Jacobins. It is possible that Atkinson put commercial interests
before political principle - he claimed that goods were still being sent to France
with government permission - but hardly likely he would harbour dangerous
foreign agents. However, Beaumont complained to Henry Dundas at the Home
Office that 'their residence in this neighbourhood is an insult to the loyal
inhabitants' and they were ordered, along with another known Republican
associate, Dillon, to leave the country. Atkinson was forced to resign his
commission.[4]

The Volunteers were in effect a Loyalist militia, and George Dyson
complained that Whitacre had attended a meeting on 9 July called to enrol a
volunteer infantry. Loyalists were not only anti-Jacobin but often intolerant of
any opponents of Church and King. George heard that

**'At Halifax a company of volunteers was drinking and the first toast was
Damnation to all dissenters and Methodists. The second toast, Down with**

all their meeting houses, chapels and conventicles, it almost makes me tremble to hear of the spirit of persecution which prevails in all the nation.'

One of the local victims of persecution, a teacher and one of George's fellow Baptists, was James Gledhill who was committed to York Castle in 1795 accused of making seditious statements. From his cell he declared why he believed a Christian should oppose the government and war;

'..that while saints are bound by the ties of Christianity to be subject to higher powers yet are they as much bound to cry against tyranny, cruelty and oppression and to mourn by their actions over the effusion of human blood.'

The repression, coupled with growing disillusionment with the bloody chaos into which France's revolutionary factions had degenerated, destroyed many of the Corresponding Societies. But the most determined Republicans were mindful of one basic right - the right to resist tyranny. [5] The involvement of Dyson and his friends highlights an important strand in the republican tradition which had its roots in the English civil war of the 1640s. Religious dissent was another way of expressing democratic social and political ideas. To natural rights and civil rights, it added the right to freedom of religious conscience, which was limited by the legislation against dissenters, such as the Test and Corporation Acts. Some nonconformists also pressed for the extension of democracy within their own sects, and the Kilhamites, who broke with the Wesleyans to form the New Connexion, were often referred to locally as the Tom Paine Methodists. Of course, not all dissenters were revolutionaries, or even radical. The congregations reflected the different political and social attitudes in the rest of society. But they encouraged people to interpret the Bible according to their own conscience, and those who were inclined could take the Christian message of salvation for the poor and humble literally. Members were also encouraged to read, express themselves in public and to organise, all skills which could be applied to political objectives. The messianic fervour sometimes generated by evangelical sermons also contributed to the atmosphere of uncertainty, and the feeling that some fundamental change was imminent. The dawning of a new century may have added to the sense of expectation, but war, shortages and epidemics meant it was not always anticipated with optimism. A Baptist, sermonizing at Quarmby in December 1800, lamented :

'He did not pretend to the knowledge of future events, but from the present state of things and from the situation of the nation it was probable that sad calamities and distresses awaited us.' [6]

TYRANTS TREMBLE THE PEOPLE ARE AWAKE
Republicans, Bread, Machinery and Peace 1798-1809

Misery due to a combination of the war and bad harvests was already apparent by the end of 1799. On Tuesday 19 November the usual concourse of people flowing into Huddersfield for market day was joined by large numbers of women from the surrounding villages. Many, it was later claimed, had already decided to attempt to seize any grain in the town, since the price of flour and meal had rocketed following the near destruction of the harvest by torrential rains. An 'immense mob' had soon congregated and Hannah Bray, the wife of a Deighton waterman, led the attack on a cart load of wheat. The intention of the rioters was not to steal the grain, but to enforce what they considered a fair price; Bray organised the sale of the bushel sacks at 6s. to women, including Emma Holland, a cloth dresser's wife, also from Deighton. At this point the magistrate, Joseph Radcliffe, appeared on the scene.

To his annoyance, several Volunteers had refused the call to arms against the crowd, and the force at his disposal was not very impressive. He read the Riot Act at several places in the town, and in reply Abraham Broadbent 'kicked his horse with the greatest violence.' Broadbent was seized along with Holland and Bray, who handed over the money she had collected to Radcliffe, commenting that she had sold it dear enough at that price. She later received a year's imprisonment in York Castle for her audacity that day, the other two receiving two or three months in the House of Correction. [1]

In March 1801 it was reported to the Home Office that secret oaths were being taken by persons in Huddersfield called Ezekielites which, although they appeared to be a religious sect, caused some alarm to the authorities due to the chilling biblical text from which the name was derived :

Ezekiel Chapter 21

> **v.26. Thus saith the Lord God: Remove the diadem and take off the crown, this shall not be the same: exalt him that is low and abase him that is high.**
> **v.27. I will overturn, overturn, overturn it, and it shall be no more until he come whose right it is and I will give it to him.**

The fanaticism of such sects, and their contempt for all man-made forms of government which they anticipated were soon to be swept away by the millenium of Christ's rule and a 'new Jerusalem,' reflected a deep disaffection from society , which, warned a government *'Secret Committee'* of inquiry, might be tapped by more down to earth revolutionaries. [2]

That same month another report from Huddersfield described an oath with overtly economic objectives, swearing persons 'to support each other in regulating and lowering the price of all necessaries of life.' The informant claimed

> **'Their proceedings are very secret and no person is informed of the particulars of the plan until he has sworn to support it and not on any account to divulge it. The people are told that they will be supported not only by numbers in all parts of the kingdom but by great folks and that the numbers will be such so suddenly called together so as to withstand any military force also that the event may take place before people in general are aware of it.'**

Despite some decreases, prices were still high and the condition of workers was aggravated by the 'extremely dead' state of trade in the town. [3]

An anonymous (and clearly written but mis-spelt) letter to Radcliffe combined complaints about the misery of the poor and the inadequacy of parish relief with biblical images.

> **'Awak Awake and Lift up your heads ye Bould Spirited Yorkshire for the Day is at hand when we shall be with you and we will find bread for both you and your Children for both Justices and Corehome [?] may quake for fear for making Mothers Disolate of their Sons and Daughters & left them to weep like so maney Reachels & will not be comforted & these hell feenes of Justices as they are have got as high as a shilling a head for the remainder of the famileys but we will restore to you your Josephs and Benjamins to old graye headed Jacob and will grant you 5s:0d. per, Head which is littele enough...'**

The threat to 'Block' (i.e. behead) the overseers of the poor and Badgers (corn dealers) concluded with a warning directed at Radcliffe, 'But no Justices shall be sparied for their hard heartedness & their Great orders.' Such threats were an occupational hazard, and probably Radcliffe did not lose much sleep over this one, despite the sinister rhyme 'Like so many Ratlers we come without the sound [of a] Drum & want radcliffe we come we come.....' ˙

The claim that '500000 are redey boys yea & stedy Boyys' is obviously a wild exaggeration - but it is just possible that the writer may have belonged to a genuine revolutionary organisation. [4]

Following the suppression of the Corresponding Societies and despite growing disillusionment with France and the terrible defeat suffered by Republicans in Ireland, hopes of a revolution still endured. Some former Corresponding Society members devoted themselves to building an underground organisation, the United Englishmen, or, later, United Britons, modelled on, and in contact with, the United Irishmen.

Republican sympathisers certainly survived in Huddersfield. In 1798 a certain John Taylor was reported to Joseph Radcliffe for drinking repeated toasts of 'Success to Buonoparte and his undertakings', in front of recruiting parties in a public house in Huddersfield. Another Taylor, George, from

Marsden, brother of the ironfounders and engineers Enoch and James, also claimed he fled the country to America in 1800 to escape persecution for his beliefs, leaving his wife and small child Robert who, 20 years later, proudly referred to himself as 'son of an exiled Radical.'

By 1800 a group of Republicans existed in Almondbury when James Gledhill of Battyeford (probably the same man imprisoned in 1795) sent a song he had composed to Edmund Norcliffe and other friends in the town to celebrate 'the coming festival' of Bastille Day. The accompanying letter showed that Republicans were hopefully struggling on despite the unfavourable political climate :

> **'in a dream a few nights ago I was in the senate house of the Gods and the Consultation of the night was how they might most effectively again reanimate Jn.Bull.... I conclude by wishing my friends an increasing stock of Patience and sensibility and you an increasing love to those philosophical Truths which beautify moral character, in the bonds of patriotic love, I am your much obliged friend...'**

The enclosed 'A patriotic song for the 14th of July 1800 being the anniversary of the French Revolution, by Citizen Gledhill...' written in the composer's ornate, cultivated hand, praised the revolution 'the bright star of freedom' and expressed hope for the liberation of all humankind:

> *Yet millions still live in the Vortex of Power*
> *Where Tyrants with cruelty reign,*
> *But quick flies old time soon will come the glad hour,*
> *When those shall their lost rights regain.*

The fact that this letter and poem was still in the possession of a member of the United Britons two years later would suggest that Gledhill's group of contacts in Almondbury, if they were not already members, certainly formed the embryo of this revolutionary organisation.

In March 1802 a delegate from Manchester, Charles Bent, visited the area and received a communication from a Wakefield and Almondbury Committee,

> **'Fellow Citizens of Manchester Committee. We the citizens of Wakefield and Almondbury Committee acting jointly being fully satisfied by the information we have received from Citizen Bent have transmitted the sum of 2.2.0. being the demand made and expenses towards our presentation to the National Committee, the Citizens of these committees return you a vote of thanks for your past favours trusting as citizens we shall have your sanction to the National Committee.'**

Bent, however, was an infiltrator, in the pay of the Bolton magistrate Colonel Fletcher, and this information was passed on to the authorities, including the name of Joseph Kaye, the head of the Almondbury division of the committee, along with others from Wakefield, Horbury and Dewsbury. It appears that the local committees had previous contact with Manchester (although any part Bent might have played in this is not revealed), but had not yet affiliated to any national organisation. Almondbury and Wakefield together claimed 645 members.[5]

Rumours of shadowy gatherings came to the magistrates' attention in 1801, including one in August on Grange Moor reported to Fitzwilliam by R.H.Beaumont. Committee men from Huddersfield, Leeds, Dewsbury, Birstall, Ardesley and elsewhere were said to be present at a meeting on Hartshead Moor but Radcliffe was not as yet too alarmed, 'I think there are but few of the disaffected United Englishmen in this neighbourhood. Saddleworth produces more being so near to the general body of them in Lancashire and the eastern part of Cheshire.' [6]

But by the following summer Radcliffe was apprehensive enough to request that troops be stationed in Huddersfield. He reported to Fitzwilliam that a 'large meeting' had been held less than two miles from his own residence at Milnsbridge House and another was to take place on the 'commons' near Honley. Some documents came into his possession in July including an extract from a pamphlet with the slogan *'Tyrants tremble the People are awake.'* outlining the aims of the United Britons :

'1st. Protect every member of the community equally in the fullest enjoyment of his natural rights from the force and injustice of any of his fellow subjects... .'

The succeeding clauses were similarly based on demands for natural justice and democratic rights, which in the United Briton's constitution were linked with more practical political proposals. Each member received a ticket bearing the motto *'Liberty, Justice and Humanity'* on which his number was written and a small eight page pamphlet containing the society's manifesto, constitution and oath. The preamble outlined the necessity of the struggle for liberty, the disastrous effects of the war and the oppression imposed on Ireland 'for no other crime than the inflexible love of Liberty...' and, above all, the need for unity. The basic aims were 'the independence of great Britain and Ireland - An equalisation of civil political and religious rights' reinforced by an oath, 'to recover those Rights which the Supreme Being in his infinite bounty has given to all men...'

The pamphlet also outlined the 'Duty of Conductors,' the officers of the society responsible for swearing in new members and forwarding names to the district executive - a system of organisation intended to combine maximum secrecy with efficient mobilisation. The titles of officers, *'Conductors'* and *'superintendents'* and the division of the membership into *'classes'* was adopted from the Methodists. The ticket received by Radcliffe bore the number '99' and, according to his information, a roll-call of numbers was held at meetings. Where the documents were found Radcliffe did not elaborate, other than that a 'gentleman' gave them to him, but investigations over the following months revealed even more evidence of the activities of the United Britons in the area.[7]

In late July Radcliffe received information of a seditious meeting at Elland, and also of two wagers that had been made by different men at different Huddersfield inns on market day, betting there would be 'a general insurrection in less than a month.' From another source he learned that one of those preparing this uprising was Joseph Halliwell of Thurstonland, a manufacturer of whisks used in cloth dressing, who, whilst travelling the manufacturing districts hawking his product, was said to be signing up men for a march on London. At Dalton he approached Christopher Stafford, a mason, and Joseph Smith, a Kirkburton farmer, asking them 'what side they were for, would they have a cake or half a cake,' assuring them 'He did not wish to take anyone's property or to hurt any man but only that everyone might have a bellyfull of meat when he had earned it.' Whether Halliwell was an official conductor of the United society or a freelance is not known, but he repeated the delusion current in some revolutionary circles that they had the backing of the Duke of Norfolk.[8]

On 24 August, General Bernard, of Heaton Lodge at Colne Bridge, received a threatening letter demanding that the numerous arms stored in his armoury for a Company of the 84th Regiment be left that night in a field for collection, or his house would be blown up. The writer's terminology makes clear his affiliation - 'may the God of heaven smile on the united company of Great Britain and Ireland and crown them with success. the tyrants tremble the people are awake...', followed by a satirical litany on the government. Bernard did not share the complacency of some of his neighbours, believing 'there is a great reason for alarm & that the country is merely deterred from rising by having troops in it...'. He complained to Fitzwilliam that Radcliffe had accepted the services of a spy, Hirst, an ex-Dragoon recently returned from Ireland, but had sent him to Bernard to be paid. Finding only his wife at home, Hirst had persuaded her to give him three guineas. Bernard also urgently wanted rid of the arms since 'I can't tell who to trust, living in the midst of the disaffected.' [9]

Around this time Lord Dartmouth got hold of a copy of the United Briton's constitution and oath, which he asked Henry Legge to promptly dispatch to the Home office. It bore the names of four of the Almondbury committee men: Joseph Kaye, David Midgeley, Sam Buckley and Tom Sykes - all of whom Radcliffe had been trying to accumulate evidence against. On 14 August, Robert Lodge, a clothier of Almondbury, was examined before the magistrate and claimed he had been admitted to the Society over a year previously by other clothiers Sam Buckley and Tom Sykes. He received a card on which was written the intitials 'DM' (David Midgeley?) and the number 50, for which he paid the subscription of one penny a week. When he refused to continue these payments he was threatened by the wife of the cordwainer, David

Midgeley. Another Almondbury witness, Mark Haigh, a yeoman farmer, said he had information from a young man who had been to a meeting of the 'Revolutioneers', and who intended getting more evidence to expose the plot. Haigh, and a merchant, Edward Harling, were said to be 'marked men' when the insurrection started, and big houses were to be raided for provisions and horses and carts to equip the march on London. For several weeks strangers had been visiting the homes of Midgeley and Buckley, and one Robert Dodson, who was seen in the latter's company at Poppleton's public house, was reported as saying 'if he had anything for his labour it would be a comfort to him but the great men of the nation would not let them reap the benefit of it....'

Radcliffe had now identified the whole committee; Buckley, the Superintendent; Sykes, the Conductor; Kaye, the secretary and Midgeley, the treasurer, whose house it was decided to raid to seize the Society's books. No membership lists were found when the authorities swooped on the 29 August - the spy Hirst learned at a meeting at Leeds that the books and tickets had been sent from Midgeley's 'to a schoolmaster at Taylor Hill'. All that was found incriminating was the letter and song of Citizen Gledhill and another, less polished, with the refrain,

> **'Rouse then Britannia, Britannia now awake,**
> **And Tyrants chains from off thee shake'.**

Significantly, according to Haigh's deposition, one of the Almondbury meetings discussed 'what were the first steps they should take - when it was concluded that they should pull down all the machinery which would return the manufacturing business to the old channel.' Whether or not this was in fact one of the objectives of the revolutionary republicans, it certainly was a question of major concern to many workers and artisans in the woollen manufacture, particularly the clothiers and cloth-dressers, or croppers. [10]

When trade unions were outlawed by the Combination Acts of 1799-1800, the Cloth Dressers' Institution became a semi-clandestine organisation, aimed at limiting the spread of machinery both by the legal means of invoking ancient laws protecting the trade, and by direct action. In 1802 there were strikes in Huddersfield against the use of gig-mills, whilst in the West Country, incendiary attacks were made on premises using the machines. The croppers' Insitution not only had a network of committees linking different towns in the West Riding but also had direct contacts with the West Country and, in December 1802, William May from Wiltshire, 'was received with the greatest kindness' by local Institution members when he visited Huddersfield. Seven croppers were imprisoned for intimidating workers who operated machines for Law Atkinson, threatening to 'gig them, as they gigged at Bradley Mill.' [11]

The fact that workers could maintain such a widespread organisation was in itself enough to alarm the authorities, but how far the members of the

Institution might have shared the aims of the UB was impossible to ascertain. Croppers were certainly not quarantined from the influences of Jacobinism. In August 1802 a Longwood cropper, William Iredale, visited Leeds and met his great-uncle, Joseph Mossley, a slubber at Gott's factory, who lived near Brown's cropping shop at Hunslet. Mossley gave William an eight page pamphlet, probably the Constitution referred to above, and told him that he had more books at his house if he called, and that meetings were held on Friday nights on Hartshead Moor. William got drunk that night and did not call for any more literature and, since he could not read much anyway, he loaned the pamphlet to a Longwood cordwainer, Abner Riley. He told his master, John Peel of Elland 'that he had got one of the books that belonged to the Revolutionists' and Peel borrowed it from him at Elland Fair.

In November, in Lambeth, the veteran republican Edward Despard was arrested at a meeting to plan the intended uprising and later that month two United Britons were arrested in Sheffield for preparing pikes. These arrests, followed by the failure of Robert Emmett's Dublin rising in July 1803, destroyed any hope of a co-ordinated revolution. The inspiration provided by France evaporated as the republican ideals of the revolution were increasingly subordinated to Bonaparte's dictatorship, while the resumption of war in 1803 also produced a wave of invasion fever not conducive to ideas still popularly regarded as pro-French. The United Societies disintegrated. In 1803 there is no evidence for the organisation in our area, but individuals continued to voice their opinions, and to suffer for it. James Jubson, a clothier, was dragged off to York, denounced by soldiers of the 18th Dragoons, for boasting that he was an ex-soldier, who had served, 'On board ship with the glorious Parker' (a leader of the Nore mutiny in 1797), and damning the king and his ministers. Ironically, the 18th Dragoons were causing more disturbance than the rebels! Three soldiers were convicted of riot and wounding following an affray at a public dance at the Nags Head, Huddersfield, in which a local man received a serious sword injury. Popular resentment towards the military was expressed in a letter John Robinson, an Elland tailor, sent to an officer of the 18th, -'the Major was then rolling in luxury and that he and the like were living on the spoil of the labouring part of the community, but that this time was short; that the writer was no enemy to the constitution in its purity but a professed enemy to tyrants and oppressors.' Robinson still clung to the remote hope of a popular uprising : 'we can raise a greater force than his Majesty or Madjesty or whatever you may please to call the Looby'. He received a year's gaol for seditious libel [12]

Agitation against machinery continued and 'mysterious' fires at Bradley Mill and Horsfalls' Ottiwells Mill in 1803 were suspected by some, though not the millowners, to be arson. A letter from Huddersfield to the London offices of the Royal Exchange Insurance Co. in 1805 did claim responsibility, warning against insuring machines - 'remember Bradley Mill in this county, which did not do one sixth of what was wished for; and expect more about December.' The threat did not materialise on this occasion, but the letter proved ominously prophetic. 'For it is ordered again to petition parliament for our rights; and if they will not grant them us by stopping the machinery belonging to us, we are determined to grant them ourselves...' To the croppers' bitter disappointment, far from sympathising with their demands, a Parliamentary Inquiry of 1806 virtually denounced the Institution as a subversive organisation. A disturbance in 1806, when gates and fences belonging to Thomas Atkinson of Bradley Mill were wrecked, may indicate continued hostility to the firm. Nine men from Birkby, Fartown and Lindley avoided prosecution by entering a 'Pardon Asked' notice in the *Leeds Mercury*. [13]

Machinery and the defence of the domestic system of production remained an important issue in the election of the Yorkshire county MPs the following year. A 'serious riot' on market day, 2 June, resulted in the injury of a number of people, damage to windows of the George Inn, and the arrest of John Cocker, an Almondbury clothier and William Hill, a labourer from Lockwood, for 'assaulting and obstructing' Radcliffe in his efforts to disperse the crowd. Along with a Lepton clothier and a Huddersfield cropper they escaped prosecution by paying costs and inserting a 'Pardon Asked' notice. Far more tolerance was shown to political violence when it was within the traditional framework of election rivalry, than when it smacked of revolutionary conspiracy.[14]

Enthusiasm for the war declined as the disruption to trade, caused by Napoleon's Berlin Decrees and parliament's retaliatory Orders in Council, increasingly affected local manufacturing. On 2 December 1807 a peace meeting was held at Honley, chaired by the wealthy methodist clothier, coalowner and farmer Tom Haigh, which asserted the loss of confidence in government ministers, condemned the calamitous war and its needless prolongation and described the economic impact - '...in consequence of the exclusion of our trade from foreign markets, our goods lay on hand, nor can we in many cases obtain remittances for those already sold.' Further meetings in Meltham and Holmfirth were followed by the 'most numerous public meeting ever held perhaps in the West Riding of this County' at Huddersfield on 1 March. An estimated 10,000 assembled before a platform including Tom Haigh, the Saddleworth manufacturer, John Platt, and Ben and Joshua Ingham. Cries of 'Peace! Peace!' greeted the reading of the resolution by the linen draper Samuel Clay. In the following weeks 20,000 signatures were collected for the peace petition.[15]

Ben Ingham, a leading Lockwood Baptist, master clothdresser, woolstapler, merchant, manufacturer and banker, was also a prominent supporter of parliamentary reform - so much so that in 1802 Joseph Halliwell had allegedly named him, along with the Duke of Norfolk, as one of the respectable backers of the revolutionary movement. On May 30 1809, along with his brother Joshua, master collier, lime-burner and banker, Samuel Clay, John Hirst, cloth dresser of Huddersfield, and Joshua Wood of Dalton, he spoke at a meeting which resolved, 'A radical Reform in the Representation of the Commons House of Parliament is therefore become absolutely necessary to the Restoration of the Constitution...'. Resolutions formulated at a London meeting of Frances Burdett were adopted and thanks voted to the veteran reformers, Cochrane, Madocks and Cartwright. Despite the respectability of the local reform leaders, the meeting was attacked in a letter from the Tory magistrate, R.H.Beaumont, to the *Leeds Intelligencer*, which dubbed it the 'Huddersfield Mob Meeting.' One accusation was that, the day after the meeting, Joshua Ingham appeared as a character witness for a Mirfield blacksmith who, on being ballotted into the militia, refused to take the oath swearing instead 'God damn King George', and whose father had told the vicar '...he would freely give a day to pull down Kings and Priests.'[16]

As events of the 1790s had shown, whilst a legal channel remained open to popular demands for political reform, the role of clandestine and insurrectionary organisations was limited. Middle class reformers like the Inghams could retain the allegiance of working class radicals. Because of the Combination Acts, economic struggles could only be conducted by a clandestine organisation, but even the croppers' Institution had concentrated its resources on openly petitioning for the enforcement of existing restrictive legislation. The conciliatory sentiments expressed in 1808, at a meeting of Huddersfield croppers, describing themselves as 'his Majesty's most faithful and loyal Subjects,' went unheeded. Acting on behalf of the merchant-manufacturers, Parliament repealed the old laws in which the croppers had placed their trust, depriving them, at a stroke, of any legal justification for continued organisation or resistance to machinery. Over the following years the introduction of shear frames and gig mills accelerated and the dislocation of trade worsened. The anonymous Luddite who penned a threatening letter in 1812 probably expressed the sentiments, if not the intentions, of many croppers as well as other workers and artisans,

'We petition no more, that wont do, fighting must.' [17]

THE METROPOLIS OF DISCONTENT
Machine Breaking and Insurrection 1812

The story of the Luddites has been told many times. But no account of rebel Huddersfield would be complete without placing Luddism in the context of the local revolutionary tradition. Luddism cannot be understood divorced from its political environment. The Luddites may not have begun their campaign as revolutionaries intent on overthrowing the government, but, as the struggle intensified, they were certainly compelled to consider a revolutionary solution. A commentator on the proceedings of the Special Commission, which tried the Luddites at York in 1813, reflected the views of the authorities when he concluded that there was a political element in local Luddism, ignited by 'the embers of revolutionary principles, which had been smouldering for several years,' earning Huddersfield notoriety as *'The metropolis of discontent'*.[1]

The first West Riding attacks in January 1812 occurred around Leeds, but it was the Huddersfield croppers who emerged as the most resolute. According to Luddite testimony, it was through the *Leeds Mercury* and 'Whig Paper' that reports of the activities of the Nottinghamshire frame-breakers came to the notice of the croppers at John Wood's cropping shop, Longroyd Bridge. After discussing these events, according to tradition, Huddersfield croppers met with those from other areas at the Shears Inn, Liversedge, and co-ordinated an attack on a cart-load of shear-frames crossing Hartshead Moor to Rawfolds Mill in early February. The first local attack was planned, under the leadership of George Mellor, Wood's step-son, for the night of Saturday 22 February. Mellor emerged as the most prominent figure in local Luddism, but it is impossible to say whether he was in fact the area's *'General Ludd'*, or just one leader unlucky enough to be caught and earn immortality by his tragic end. Meetings with other croppers, as well as those at the nearby Fisher's cropping shop, took place before the night. One cropper was emboldened enough to nearly give the game away. At Moldgreen, the Friday before the attack, Mark Hill threatened John Walker, as he was carting shear-frames from Lockwood to Almondbury, promising that within a week the machines would be broken. [2]

At eleven o'clock on the Saturday night 45 men assembled in a field at Rashcliffe belonging to John Wood. A decision had been made to bring firearms, and some may have been familiar with drill since the party was formed into three companies, 'but the system was yet in its infancy they had not above eleven guns and pistols that night'. After an hour it was decided that everyone who was intending to come had arrived, and there was some disappointment that there were fewer than expected. Joseph Drake was sent as a scout to see if a party had assembled on Crosland Moor. After some discussion, it was decided not to attack Bradley Mill. It would have been a hard nut to crack for a first attempt, considering, both 'the well known courage of the owner,' Tom Atkinson and the size of the premises. Instead it was agreed to attack smaller cropping shops. The men were given numbers before marching off.

It was a moonlit night. The gunmen were the first to approach Joseph Hirst's shop at Marsh where a man and two boys were still up working. Admittance was demanded and the gunmen stood guard, while the shears were broken with a hammer. As pistols were fired off both inside and out of the buildings (some shots hitting the master's dog) there was a call for silence. It was decided that the machinery was not adequately broken and it took another ten minutes of furious hammering before the seven frames and 24 pairs of shears were smashed. Outside someone said 'Now for the windows' and three were broken before 'one called the general and a person disguised' told them to leave them alone. In reply to the call 'Now for the house and master' orders were issued to let them alone too - unless they had to return, then - 'We'll do it to the bottom.'

Via Longroyd Bridge, the party then marched to Crosland Moor where James Balderstone used machinery 'not upon a large scale but on the most domestic and contemptible one,' having only one frame. Balderstone was awakened by the attempted entry. A voice said they only wanted a light for a candle, but he replied with a threat to shoot them. The door was broken open and, while the husband and wife were held at gunpoint, the Luddites rushed upstairs and broke the frame and eight pairs of shears. On leaving, at about two in the morning, a gun was fired. Amongst those later denounced for their prominent part in this and successive Luddite operations were Ben Walker, who had a gun and had done the breaking; George Mellor, armed with a scythe-blade sword and pistol; William Thorpe; Tom Smith, a hatchet man; Joshua Schofield, who kept watch; George Lodge, described as 'sergeant', wearing a white sash; George Brook; Jonathan Dean, carrying a hatchet or hammer; John Walker and Lawrence Gaffney. Only the latter was to escape arrest, fleeing, it was suspected to Ireland, from where, as his name suggests, he may have originated. [3]

On a dark and rainy night of 5-6 March the Luddites met at the ironically named Dry Clough Lane, near Lockwood, where men from Dalton arrived so drenched that they returned home, leaving only 16 to participate in the raids. They were guided to the house of Sam Swallow at Linthwaite by one of the croppers. Arriving in the early hours of the morning they demanded entry and smashed four pairs of shears, two shear-frames and a brushing machine, whilst the householder was guarded by a man with a pistol in one hand and a candle in the other. On departing they bade him good morning. An apprentice of Wood pilfered an axe, marked with an 'S', which, according to the Luddite informant, William Hall, was beaten out on the stove at the cropping shop. Hall also later described one of the attackers as John Walker, who 'had a pistol and a most terrible mask made out of a red and white spotted calf skin.' At the work-shop of William Cotton, Linthwaite, ten pairs of shears and one brushing machine were broken and a gun taken. A threat was made to blow up the premises if they found machinery there again .[4]

George Roberts, of South Crosland, was the next target. On 13 March, not long after midnight, Roberts heard knocking at the door. Asked what they wanted, someone replied 'We'll let you see what we want', and, as he opened the door, a number of men rushed in, disguised with blackened faces or black cloth masks with eye and mouth holes. He remonstrated that he had taken down all his shear frames and begged them not to break his shears. Someone ordered 'Go forward,' but he begged them again and they promised, if the frames had been dismantled, not to smash the shears. Whilst they searched upstairs he was held at pistol point by a masked man, and made to sit on a piece laid out on the house floor. He gave them the key to the barn where the frames were stored and, after two were broken, pistols were pointed at his head to reinforce a threat to blow out his brains if they were set up again. His wife was also warned by a man with a white napkin round his face, that if her father didn't dismantle his frames they would go to Marsden the next week with 400 men.

The party, about 30 strong, then proceded to Honley, where John Garner was disturbed by a noise outside, and voices saying 'watch the windows, take care of the windows.' After a burst of apparently ineffective hammering someone commented 'If thou can't use that maul better give it me.' His dressing shop was entered, and two shear frames and seven shears broken, along with the tumbling shafts and drums for working the frames. The attackers stole his pistol and, as they marched off, a shot was fired. By around half past two the Luddites had reached Lockwood. Hannah, the wife of Clement Dyson, was wakened by a great noise. The intruders were let in, and two frames, one brushing machine, seven shears, tubs and other utensils were broken. Some of the men demanded drink but did not partake when it was offered.

These attacks were against small master dressers and relatively low risk for the Luddites. However, on the evening of 15 March, a far more daring operation was carried out on the premises of Frank Vickerman, a large merchant manufacturer. A letter thrown into his premises proved no idle threat:

> **'We give you Notice when the Shers is all Broken the Spinners shall be the next if they be not taken down vickerman tayler Hill he has had is Garde but we will pull all down som night and kill him that Nave and Roag'.**

Although the Committee of Merchants and Manufacturers, set up on 23 February to suppress the Luddites - and on which Vickerman sat - had secured the billetting of two troops of dragoons in the town to provide patrols and guards to protect Vickerman's Taylor Hill premises, the Luddites planned an attack with military precision.[5]

One cropper, Joseph Drake, was at Methodist Chapel the night before, when he was told by John Walker of 'a bit of a maneouvre on Taylor Hill.' Drake and Walker's job was to observe Brooks Corner at Huddersfield, where the guard for Vickerman assembled, and alert the attacking party to the progress of troops by pistol shots. George Mellor had also, over a drink at Wood's cropping shop, arranged with three young lads who served as Huddersfield Church bell-ringers, one of them a cousin of the Luddite William Thorpe, to act as signallers. Someone was to run to tell them as soon as the military piquet rode out, and they promised to have the bells ready to strike off at once.

The guard usually reached Taylor Hill around nine. The Luddites assembled about half a mile away in Pricking Wood on the valley side above Lockwood Spa. Some were late to arrive, so there was no time for the usual roll-call, and the party reached Vickerman's by about half past eight. The cropping shop and the dwelling house were in the same building, which was surrounded and entry forced. This was the most destructive attack so far, indicating a particular hostility to Vickerman. As well as the ten frames and thirty shears, a clock was smashed, and Mellor put the blade of his scythe sword through every pane of glass in the dressing shop. Wool and cloth were also thrown over the stove in an attempt to start a fire. As Huddersfield church bells began to peal, followed by shots, someone commanded 'Out! Out!' Guns were emptied into the house before they left. Meanwhile, after the bells rang out, the further progress of the patrol past Chapel Hill was marked by a shot. Walker was to relay a shot from Knowle Hill, but as his pistol misfired, he had to rush into the nearby house of Joseph Sowden and grab a red-hot poker to detonate the charge.

Apparently only Huddersfield men were involved, but the more ambitious nature of the operation presaged the next phase of the campaign when large mills were attacked. How far links had been built up with croppers in neighbouring areas at this time is not clear, but by April attempts at wider co-ordination are evident.[6]

A small group ranged the Holme Valley from Snowgate Head to Honley on 5 April, destroying frames and shears at three shops, but only four days later an attack was launched in an entirely new direction and on a quite different scale. On 9 April the assault on Foster's mill at Horbury was said to involve 300 men, which, even allowing for exaggeration, would indicate more than the usual twenty to forty. Since a 'very great number' was seen crossing Grange Moor it was believed that the majority were from the Huddersfield area, while others appeared from the Wakefield direction. Over £291 damage was done, not only to the dressing shop but to the scribbling mill, woollen warps and window frames. The co-ordination of Luddites from different areas for a large scale attack was attempted two days later at Cartwright's mill at Rawfolds, Liversedge, but without success. George Wilson, a Luddite sympathiser living in Saddleworth who was in touch with Nottingham, recounted that the 'Luds was defeated which was owing to Halifax Luds not coming up as they were appointed...'. This failure led to acrimony between Huddersfield and Halifax Luddites which was still remembered five years later. Two of the attackers were killed and many wounded in a 20 minute exchange of fire with the mill's defenders.[7]

It was reputed to be have been as a direct result of the losses sustained by the Luddites at Rawfolds that Mellor resolved 'there was no method of smashing the machinery, but by shooting the masters.' A few weeks later an anonymous letter, purporting to come from 'Peter Plush Secretary to General Ludd' senior at Nottingham to General Ludd junior at Huddersfield, expressed approval of an attempt to shoot Cartwright on 18 April. It too advocated vengeance. 'The General further informs me to say that he trusts to the attachment of his subjects for the avenging of the death of the two brave youths who fell at the deye of Rawfold...' But as well as encouraging assassination it also locates the local Luddite struggle in a wider political context - the devising of a 'grand attack' against the government and monarchy.

'I am further authorised to say that it is the opinion of our general and men that as long as that blackguard drunken whoring fellow called Prince regent and his servants have anything to do with government that nothing but distress would befole us his foot stooles...it is expected that you will remember that you are made of the same stuff as Georg Gwelps Juner and corn and wine are sent for you as well as him.'

Over the following months machine breaking was abandoned as the Luddites embarked on a campaign both of individual terror against local opponents and also the seizure of arms in preparation of an uprising. There are indications that they considered themselves part of a growing revolutionary movement, although evidence of concrete links is slim, and that the movement, partly at least, was motivated by Republican ideas.[8]

Most of the evidence for Luddite ideology comes from anonymous sources like the 'Peter Plush' letter, and although we have no proof that the writers of such documents actually participated in attacks, they certainly reveal a knowledge of the tactics and intended targets of the Luddites. Inasmuch as their authors breathed the same social and political atmosphere as the machine-breakers, and articulated ideas which were current amongst them, they can be considered genuine Luddite documents. One of the earlier letters reflects Luddism at its least political, explaining, also in the name of *'Soliciter to General Ludd'*, that the croppers of the Huddersfield District had spent £7,000 vainly petitioning against machinery 'so they are trying this method now.' It made the assurance that there was no other purpose 'for as soon as the obnoxious machinery is stoped or distroyed the General and his Brave Army will be disbanded and return to their Employment like other Liege Subjects.' Nevertheless, the 'Soliciter' was not averse to threatening to burn down Radcliffe's house, with him in it, if he continued to oppose them, adding, with a hint of Jacobin terminology, 'for our Court is not Govern'd by Sovrns [Sovereigns] but Equity.' [9]

Despite obvious exaggerations, a letter sent to George Smith (whose machinery was smashed on 5 April), is more explicitly political. After warning Smith to take down his frames, it claimed 'there were 2,782 Sworn Heroes bound in a Bond of Necesity' in the 'Army of Huddersfield' and that they were in touch with other West Riding towns, the cotton country and Scotland, which were ready to rise along with the Papists in Ireland and the help of the French 'so that they are likely to find the soldiers something else to do than idle in Huddersfield and then Woe be to the places now guarded by them...' Although there is no evidence for actual revolutionary preparations at this time - and certainly not on the scale described in the letter (the intention of the writer being to intimidate), it does show that the idea of insurrection was not alien in some Luddite circles. It must have been apparent to the Luddites that just such a rising would indeed assist their struggle. One letter written in the name of General Ludd in Leeds, is explicitly Republican in content, 'all Nobles and Tyrants must be put down, come let us follow the example of the Brave Citizens of Paris...', whilst the Huddersfield Manufacturers' Committee '*Wanted*' posters were countered by graffiti on walls and doors, offering 100 guineas for the Prince Regent's head. The plausibility of the circulation of Republican ideas among Luddites is substantiated by the finding of a copy of the decade old Constitution of the United Britons, dropped during the attack on Foster's mill. [10]

Following the failure at Rawfolds, as Luddism developed into a revolutionary movement and extended its base, other workers and artisans were drawn in, including Jacobin elements. One of these was the Halifax hatter, John Baines, a Republican for twenty years, who was in contact with Luddism even before the Rawfolds attack, since one of his associates, a cardmaker, Charles Milnes, claimed to know the two killed there 'very well'.

The attacks on individuals targeted not only notorious machine users but also other opponents of the movement. When Cartwright was shot at the week following the attack on his mill, the military did not consider it the work of isolated gunmen, since lights and signal shots were used to decoy troops from the area. The house at Paddock of the Huddersfield constable George Whitehead, was shot into on 15 April. Ben Walker, the informer, later said that George Mellor had planned to attack Milnsbridge House itself, but that only

Mellor, an apprentice and himself arrived at the rendezvous. It was on the way home from this aborted operation that Mellor shot at Whitehead with a pistol loaded with bone fragments. However, Walker could have got this detail from the *Mercury* report of the incident. On 23 April, Isaac Raynor, one of Radcliffe's farmworkers, returning home to Linthwaite from Milnsbridge, was shot at by three men, though it is not clear whether this was an opportunistic attack or whether they were awaiting him. Radcliffe received a letter about this time warning that machinery would lead to civil war, and that Tom Atkinson of Bradley Mill and William Horsfall of Ottiwells Mill would 'soon be numbered with the dead.' On 28 April Horsfall was fatally wounded at Crosland Moor, less than a mile from Radcliffe's residence.[11]

The first recorded arms raid took place the following night. Clement Dyson, the cloth dresser of Dungeon whose frames had already been smashed, was roused by knocking on the door and the command 'General Ludd has sent us for your gun and pistol and we must have them immediately.' He replied, 'I have the gun in my hand - and if any man enters my house he shall have the contents of it.' Warned, 'If you shoot anyone, yourself and your family will be corpses in ten minutes' his wife hastily put a gun and pistol out of the door. Dyson thought that 20 to 30 men were involved. On 1 May Joshua Brook at New Gate, Wooldale, also received callers who announced that General Ludd had sent them for arms, and his double-barrelled pistol was taken. Over the following week raids were reported in several villages and about 100 stand of arms were taken by bands of 20 to 50 men. A month later arms were being taken almost every night, whilst lead pipes and dyeing utensils mysteriously disappeared, presumably, the authorities assumed, for moulding into bullets. In July a pistol was taken from the Holmfirth attorney, Cookson Stephenson, by men who took 'a courteous leave', while in Almondbury, the party which took the gun of clothier Joseph North, marched off in military order led by a mounted man. As well as affecting the Huddersfield area, particularly around Holmfirth, raids occurred at Horbury, Elland, Stainland and Clifton.[12]

The *Leeds Mercury* commented on the fact that nothing other than arms were stolen in the May and early June raids until, on 13 June, money was taken. This does not necessarily indicate, as was the case in December, that gangs of housebreakers were operating under the guise of Luddism. Taking money was apparently justified on the grounds that it was needed for the intended uprising. At Briestwhistle on 23 June the leader of the party ordered the release of the householder 'Let him go,don't hurt him, we have got what we wanted and we will bring it back in three months.' In a raid at Kirkheaton, when the owner said his gun had been taken to the guardhouse for security, cash was demanded instead, 'We are to have a fight soon and will endeavour to let you have your money after it is over.'[13]

One gentleman reporting to Fitzwilliam on the Luddite attack at Clifton on 13 July could not conceal his admiration of:

'the precision, intrepidity and dispatch with which an armed banditti regularly searched a populous village a mile in length for arms and took away six or seven, without attempting to touch other property, firing repeatedly into houses and at individuals who attempted the least resistance with a promptitude and apparent discipline that no regular troops could exceed.' [14]

Attacks on individuals continued. The house of the constable, Milnes, at Lockwood, was shot into, whilst John Blythe of Holmfirth received death threats. Radcliffe continued to be the target of threats and he rarely ventured out. On 22 July John Hinchliffe, a clothier of Upperthong and parish clerk at Holmfirth church, was shot and badly wounded as a suspected informer. This case revealed the political strategy now motivating the Luddites. In May Hinchliffe had been approached by an acquaintance, John Schofield of Netherthong, who offered to 'twist him in', that is, administer the illegal oath admitting him to the movement since 'They wanted a body of men at Holmfirth - they had got one at Huddersfield and wanted one at all places - and then it might all start in a moment and every place might do its own and overturn the government.' Hinchliffe later related this to the Rev. Keeling, who passed on the information to Constable Blythe. Allegedly it was Blythe's threat to arrest Schofield which provoked the assassination attempt. [14]

The widespread use of 'twisting-in' to recruit men into the movement is evident from the record of the counter-insurgency campaign in the manufacturing districts, compiled by Captain Francis Raynes of the Stirlingshire Militia. Raynes devised a system of highly mobile night patrols and secret agents to try to infiltrate the Luddites. Particular targets were those most active in administering the oath, the 'twisters'. The oath he describes, and the recollections of it in the depositions of witnesses, is similar to a version forwarded from Manchester to Radcliffe in early April. After being twisted-in, those willing to swear in others were given a hand-written version of the oath which, in the course of transmission became corrupted. Thus in the copy used by the weaver Craven Cookson and John Eadon at Barnsley, the phrase 'to the verge of Nature' becomes 'to the verge of *Statude*.' (Raynes records it as 'verge of Existence.') The threat of 'being put out of the world by the first brother whom I may meet' in the event of treachery by the oath-taker, was sufficiently chilling to be remembered by Hinchliffe as part of the oath shown to him by Schofield, and by William Hall in the one George Mellor made him swear. The spread of twisting-in beyond the ranks of the croppers proves clearly that it was not a purely machine-breaking organisation which was being created. Schofield certainly understood it to have political objectives and Eadon at Barnsley said the oath 'was to form a regular organisation in the country to overturn the tyrannical system of government', whilst, if the testimony of the police agent Macdonald can be believed, John Baines at Halifax gave the oath only to those who understood the words 'Democracy' and 'Aristocracy'. [16]

According to the arrested Wooldale carpenter and Militia corporal, Joseph Barrowclough, who turned informer, the Luddites also called themselves 'the Godly', and used a quote from Ezekiel 21:26. Unfortunately Barrowclough's evidence can be given little credence - Hay, the Stockport magistrate who interrogated him, concluded that he was 'somewhat light in his upper regions' - and his detailed evidence about arms caches proved fictitious, although based on accurate descriptions of the locations. However, like the knowledge of the supposed hiding places for weapons, it may contain an element of reality in that there was a recollection of the Ezekielite oath of 1801 still current.

The oath was obviously instrumental in building a movement with a political objective - but how far was this movement organised for a co-ordinated attack on the state? Radcliffe received a copy of "delegates orders" from an unnamed source which described in detail a secret system of communication and the widespread preparation of pikes from London to Carlisle. Unfortunately the doubtful origin of this document must cast suspicion on its reliability. Although the authorities believed that clandestine meetings composed of delegates from other areas were taking place, such as one held at the *Cross Pipes* on Denby Moor during Shepley Feast in June, no hard evidence was uncovered. However, considering that workers were experienced at operating illegally - it was less than a decade since the croppers' Institution had functioned with a wide network of delegates and committees - it is quite feasible that the level of organisation was more complex than that revealed by investigations.

There is no evidence for the unlikely claim made by local historian Frank Peel, that the Nottinghamshire Luddite, George Weightman, addressed croppers at the Shears Inn, but there is evidence for other individuals maintaining links between different areas. A framework knitter in Uppermill, Saddleworth, was revealed to be a Nottingham Luddite, both in communication with Manchester and knowledgeable about the Rawfolds attack, while a spy in Saddleworth, investigating the suspect Joseph Kenworthy, found that the '...chief rendezvous for him and his associates is at Long Royd Bridge.' This was more than three weeks before the arrest of George Mellor and the other croppers from there. Kenworthy himself was suspected of being involved in the shooting of Horsfall, since he was absent from home at the time, and his family had been supplied with 'plenty of provisions' from a source in Huddersfield. Kenworthy made his living dealing in second-hand wool cards and had a legitimate reason for travelling around the manufacturing districts without any sinister motives. On the other hand, such an occupation would provide ideal cover for a real delegate of a subversive organisation. Information on contact with Luddism further afield was given by George Howarth whom John Lloyd, clerk to the Stockport magistrates but also active in tracking suspects around Huddersfield, described as coming from High Burton.   When Howarth took advantage of the government amnesty, first offered in August, to become '*un-twisted*' by recanting the Luddite oath and taking one of loyalty, he claimed he had been sworn in by Tom Whittaker of Cheshire, transported for administering illegal oaths. If he is the George Howorth [sic], suspected by Acland of being a former member of a 'secret committee' from Lancashire or Cheshire, now supposed to be working near Rastrick, it could indicate the extent of hidden links. Lloyd also reported that some others taking the oath of allegiance said they had been twisted-in by Edmund Newton, an arrested Lancashire suspect, although he did not specify whether these were from the Huddersfield or Saddleworth area. [17]

The mythical figure of General Ludd epitomised the nature of the movement which, while lacking real central leadership and direction, was bound together in common resistance to both the changing economic order and the government. 'General Ludd' expressed the aspirations of large numbers of workers and artisans who might not themselves be directly involved in armed actions. In effect, Luddism was a popular resistance movement, opposed to the growing domination of industrial capitalism and its political guardians which, although the croppers were the driving force, was not restricted to a single occupational group. Even in the West Riding, the machine breaking aspect was not restricted merely to shear-frames. Radcliffe complained that, on 9/10 May, within a mile of his own residence, 'an attack of destruction was made on another description of machinery', when a scribbling mill was broken in to. In April, a threshing machine and barn was destroyed by a group of masked men at Carlton near Barnsley, the following month one at Dewsbury was burned down whilst, in August, a farmer near Rastrick was ordered by raiders to dismantle his. Luddism's initial strength, but ultimate weakness, was that it was basically a spontaneous movement, drawing in people variously motivated by hostility to machinery, economic grievances (taxes, low wages or high prices) and political discontent with the government. Although the first two struggles were increasingly channelled into the latter, there was not sufficient clarity of aims to create an effective revolutionary strategy and maintain an organisation capable of withstanding repression. [18]

The Luddites saw themselves as a paramilitary force, an 'Army of Redressers' as they called themselves, and, like any other guerilla fighters, they could not have survived as an underground group for as long as they did without the support of their own community. This was vital to their survival, and there is ample evidence that the Luddites attracted substantial support beyond the ranks of journeyman croppers directly threatened with displacement by machinery and not only from working class members of their communities. A number of master croppers who saw the danger machinery posed to domestic industry indicated support for Luddism. Joseph Ardron of Dalton took the risk of helping one of his workers, James Haigh, wounded at Rawfolds, to go into hiding with Ardron's friends at Penistone and his mother at Willow Bridge. Francis Vickerman thought that the 'spirit of rebellion [was] promoted in this neighbourhood chiefly by men who Imploy four or five to twenty men who can in general get great wages and spend more at the ale house than all the other inhabitants.' He named two master dressers, Joseph Beaumont and William Hargreaves of Lockwood as 'the leaders looked up to and regulate the secret organisations...' After the arrest of Mellor and his comrades an anonymous informant, *'A Friend to Peace,'* claimed that Beaumont and Hargreaves, along with another Lockwood master cropper, George Richardson, a woolstapler, Thomas Ellis and John Wood, Mellor's stepfather, were arranging defence witnesses and comprised the 'principal agitators' in the district. Since Mellor did indeed write to Ellis from his cell there is apparently some basis for this information. The number of respectable witnesses prepared to come forward to testify to the character of some of the defendants also reflects the level of approval they had in the community. [19]

It took many months of constant questioning, offers of rewards - as much as £2000, an enormous sum in 1812 - and threats of punishment, including hanging, before the authorities obtained any useful information. Certainly, the oath taken by the Luddites was held in high regard, and kept many of them silent even under sentence of death - it was seen as their only protection and guaranteed solidarity in the face of the overwhelming power of the authorities. Others remained silent from fear - not just fear of possible Luddite reprisals, but fear of the reaction of other members of their close knit communities, if it became known that they had given information. This reflects the fact that large numbers of people identified with the Luddite cause and were prepared to support it. The Huddersfield area in 1812 comprised small communities, in which it would have been impossible for anyone to hide from their neighbours the kind of nocturnal activities in which the Luddites were involved. Comings and goings would be heard and known about by those who lived nearby. Many people must have realised the identity of those involved in machine breaking, but, far from giving information to the authorities, the ordinary people chose to protect them by silence.

On 9 May the *Leeds Mercury* reported 'We believe there is a very general disposition among the lower classes to view the actions of the persons engaged in this association with complacency, not to say with approbation. This is the strength and life's blood of the association.' Only a week before, the magistrate, Joseph Scott of Woodsome, had written to the Home Secretary in similar vein 'it is too manifest that the great body of the lower orders of people are either participants in the Great Abbettors of the cause or intimidated into submission', whilst Lloyd noted later that the Luddite 'system' 'met with countenance from most of the lower orders.' After the Rawfolds attack, it was noted that members of the crowd which gathered at the mill 'expressed their regret that the attempt had failed'.[20]

Support was not only passive. The croppers set up a fund to support those wounded at Rawfolds and their families. John Bates of Holmfirth, who may be the prominent local reformer of that name, subscribed a guinea - a week's wage for a cropper - while John Schofield, later suspected of John Hinchliffe's shooting, gave 11s. The respectable sum of £8.14s.6d. was handed over by Ben Hinchliffe to Mark Hill, the Moldgreen cropper later arrested for his part in the attack. If this Hinchliffe was the one subsequently arrested for arms stealing, then he was only a labourer, and the money must have been collected from sympathisers. A more violent demonstration of popular sentiment in support of Luddism occurred at the beginning of May when a woman in one unnamed village near Huddersfield, who had been to the magistrates on a totally unconnected case, was stoned and nearly killed as a suspected informer. At the end of September a patrol was 'pelted' at Lockwood and in October a group of locals disrupted a soldier's wedding party at an Elland pub. At Lindley, a labourer, cloth dresser and four masons were arrested for an attack on a patrol, in which a soldier was struck on the head by a stone and badly injured. The popular opposition in Lindley may have been behind the refusal of one publican, Waterhouse, to billet troops on his premises. Radcliffe feared that the presence of soldiers in the 'small alehouses of this neighbourhood' could become a flashpoint for a punch-up with the locals, or worse, 'if drunkeness is looked upon as an excuse for making seditious statements.' Captain Raynes detected an improvement in the mood of the natives when his men were no longer spat on and people in pubs became 'more inclined to be civil.'[21]

The authorities avoided calling out the Agbrigg Militia because it was feared that local men would not pursue the Luddites enthusiastically, whilst militia units brought into the area were moved around frequently, in order to prevent them from being tainted with Luddite ideas. That this was not an unfounded fear was shown by the soldier of the Cumberland Militia at Cartwright's mill, court-martialled and flogged for refusing to fire, according to tradition 'lest I might hit some of my brothers.' This soldier may have known nothing first hand of the problems of the croppers, but he must have been aware of the sufferings of the working class in general and it was not uncommon for militia men called out on riot duty to show sympathy in this way. Samuel Hartley, one of the Luddite fatalities at Rawfolds, was also a private in the Halifax Militia - the same regiment in which Cartwright was a Captain.[22]

One of the most remarkable manifestations of public sympathy was shown at Luddite funerals. Hartley was given a magnificent ceremony in Halifax and 'great numbers' of people gathered in Huddersfield to give John Booth a similar send-off. The authorities, alarmed by the demonstration at Hartley's funeral, pre-empted any plans by burying Booth secretly at 6 am, angering many who wished to show their respects. Scenes of near-riot occurred when some of those hanged in 1813 were refused burial by Methodist ministers, and many people accompanied the bodies along part of the sad route back from York, or greeted them on their arrival at Huddersfield, the numbers swelling to thousands as the waggons proceeded along Leeds Road. [23]

Respect for the Luddites was not confined to the local population, as their executions bore witness. In 1812 public hangings were a popular form of entertainment, accompanied as any fair would be, by ballad sellers, refreshment hawkers and general scenes of mirth and merriment to be enjoyed by the vast throngs who gathered. The Luddite hangings provided a stark contrast. Enormous numbers did gather, but they watched solemnly. They listened to and joined in the prayers and hymn singing, another unusual feature, - but showed none of the signs of enjoyment associated with such events. Their silence and grief were surely an indication of sympathy and a feeling that these young men at least did not deserve to die for their 'crimes'. The *York Herald* reporter, possibly no stranger to such spectacles, never before saw spectators with "more pity depicted on the human countenance." [24]

The fringes of Luddism also attracted some rogue characters whose actual involvement is not clear, but their readiness to express sympathy for the Ludds indicates the popularity of the movement. Patrick Doring, an Irish quack doctor residing at Scholes, was gaoled for two years after threatening Joseph and Martha Culpan, who had sheltered the wounded James Haigh, that they would be shot if they gave any information. Four years later Doring, alias 'Dr Bell' was again in trouble when he fled the country accused of the rape of 14 year old Ann Broadbent. Unflatteringly described as five feet six inches tall, with a fresh complexion, flattish nose, brown hair and with a 'cast of the mouth when he speaks', the authorities pursued him with unusual vigour and after five months on the run he was apprehended in Newry, Ireland, by George Whitehead the Huddersfield deputy constable. On 12 April the following year he went to the gallows at York. [25]

One of the suspects named by Barrowclough as a delegate may have had genuine Luddite connections. Robert Harling, a hawker who lodged somewhere near Honley, was picturesquely depicted as 'about 30 years of age, five foot eight or nine inches high, lame in one of his hands, thin and rather fair of complexion, has an effeminate voice, mostly carries a basket slung over his shoulder and goes about the country selling spices...' It is possible that he was the Honley cropper of that name, gaoled at Rothwell the previous year as an insolvent debtor. Arrested for administering unlawful oaths he was remanded in York Castle and there implicated a young cropper, Cornelius Hobson, as the twister-in from whom he had received the oath. Hobson was also mentioned by John Bates when he was interrogated. Another Harling, also a hawker, Samuel of Crosland Moor, was apprehended for threatening the life of Radcliffe, after declaring in a pub at Stockport that he was a 'damned rascall' and that he 'would be damned if he lived long, for he would give him a pill', that is, a bullet. But since he was 69 years old and partially infirm, it is hard to see what threat he posed. His prosecution, like the other Harling's and Hobson's, was later dropped, much to the annoyance of Radcliffe, who seemed to grow even more vindictive as Luddite activity declined. [26]

Another Crosland Moor man who allegedly planned to kill Radcliffe was still under surveillance two years later. Thomas Riley, a 55 year old tailor was informed on by his apprentice, William Hobson of Lockwood, who claimed that a few weeks after the Rawfolds fight his master said there were some tyrants 'whose lives must be put an end to, that if Mr Radcliffe was killed this country would be infinitely pleased.' Hobson was asked to join a group of men to make up a dozen. When he refused he was warned not to tell anyone or 'if thou dost thou will be shot for thou knows what's going forward.' He was not approached again, but at work he frequently heard Riley wish that Radcliffe be assassinated. It was two years before he made his deposition to the magistrates. Riley did not abandon his plan when he failed to recruit Hobson. In July he called on John Drake of Longroyd Bridge, whom he told of a proposal to get together 40 or 50 Ludds for an attack on Milnsbridge House, disarm the guards and kill Radcliffe. His admission that he could not take part in murder himself probably did little for his credibility. According to John's son Joseph, Riley was often coming out with plans to attack mills and destroy machinery. Sarah, John's wife recollected Riley saying Radcliffe was 'a tyrant upon the earth and a Blood sucker' who 'would drain the country of all true Britons'. and that he suggested drawing the troops away with a false report about a meeting 'upon the Blackmoor' and then seizing Radcliffe's guard. Riley may have had no actual influence whatsoever on Luddite operations but he was taken seriously enough by the authorities and cannot be dismissed as a crank, although, as we shall see, he does appear to have suffered from mental instability when his schemes led him into serious trouble five years later. Since in 1817 he certainly was in contact with genuine revolutionaries, it is possible that in 1812 he was also involved with Luddites and, if this Joseph Drake is the cropper who was involved in the attacks on Vickerman's and Rawfolds, then Riley's proposition to him and his father about a raid on Milnsbridge House does not appear so ridiculous. [27]

The popularity of the Luddites certainly did encourage some idiosyncratic behaviour. In April a Mr Beswick was arrested in Huddersfield for claiming to be General Ludd. Described as of some 'opulence', he was released when the authorities ascertained it was 'not the first dilemma into which he has precipitated himself by his eccentricity.' William Sykes, a Meltham shopkeeper, had a narrower escape when he ended up at York assizes for demanding arms in the name of General Ludd from a neighbour's house one night. Luckily the jury were convinced that it was only a drunken prank.[28]

If the general populace supported the Luddites, what was their attitude to those in authority whose avowed intention was the destruction of the Luddite cause ? It is hard to imagine a community, except one engaged in civil war, more divided by mutual hostility. Of the manufacturers, Francis Vickerman appears to have been particularly detested - not only were his premises attacked with unusual virulence but, a leading Methodist, he was nicknamed 'the Bishop' and was publicly derided in 'a song of ridicule'. Whether his unpopularity predated Luddism, or resulted from his prominence in the Manufacturers Committee is not clear. It may have been known that he regularly passed on information about his neighbours which could have led to their arrest. Although already a prime target, he feared exposure of his role as an informer. At the beginning of July, Lloyd reported to Radcliffe that, at Chester, he had met Vickerman who was 'alarmed that it should be known he has anything to do with me.' He is probably the 'Mr V' who supplied details implicating Joseph Mellor's 'brother' in Horsfall's murder. Under his own name he also sent a list of names to General Acland, including that of Ben Walker.[29]

Cartwright became either a recluse or an outcast after the Rawfolds affair, and would never speak of the night on which two men died. As for Horsfall, though much was made at the trials of the affection in which he was held by his men, Colonel Campbell reported how, as he lay wounded, a crowd gathered and reproached him with being an oppressor of the poor, while his assassins were allowed to escape into the wood. This report was included in the Committee of Secrecy findings in 1812, but was never otherwise alluded to. It is unlikely that a popular man would have been reviled as he lay dying. Whether he was really loved amongst his own workers is also doubtful. Some did assist him in guarding Ottiwells Mill, but even one of these, George Williams, fell victim to Horsfall's suspicious temper, and was attacked one night by his master who believed that he was a Luddite. Williams later recalled the curious fact that, the day Horsfall was shot, the mill was finishing its first ever order of black cloth. [30]

But perhaps the greatest hostility was reserved for Radcliffe, the man whose tireless efforts to smash the Luddites eventually led to his being awarded a Baronetcy. He himself felt that he had been a prisoner in his own home for over ten months, and admitted that the 'odium of the disaffected' put a burden on the members of his family, 'My daughters never walk out of my grounds without receiving insults'. Protected by soldiers, he constantly suffered abuse and threats. One of those accused of uttering threats, Sam Harling, was also expressing popular opinion when he said that Radcliffe 'would not do justice to anyone who came before him.' This view is confirmed by the fact that when, after the trials, men came forward to take the oath of allegiance none of them went to Radcliffe, preferring Scott, or another magistrate, who had not been so ruthless in tracking down Luddites. Following the October arrests, threats against him increased. 'Enemie Anonimous' vowed revenge, promising to make himself 'another Bellingham', a reference to the assassin of Prime Minister Perceval, whilst 'Secretary to the Brotherhood', claiming that despite the arrests, 'we have thousands in the neighbourhood left', notified Radcliffe that he would be dead by 2 January 1813. Radcliffe survived, though his residence was shot into in January. The threats and general hostility undoubtedly took their toll and he developed some kind of nervous 'shake', which increasingly affected the legibility of his writing and, no doubt, his mental well-being. By June 1813, he was proposing to 'retire to some more peacable part of the Kingdom.' It seems difficult to imagine how any of those so deeply involved in putting down the Luddites could live comfortably within their own communities even when the movement was over. [31]

Whilst the bulk of the population were at odds with the authorities relations between the different arms of the state were not very harmonious either. Radcliffe and Lloyd were often at loggerheads attested to by numerous acrimonious letters. General Maitland, the commander of the army in the North, had little time for either of them. He abhorred Lloyd's brutal tactics for obtaining information, whilst finding the results extremely useful. Radcliffe he regarded as a pompous, neurotic and self-important bore, unfortunately useful and necessary in the fight against Luddism. As he complained to Acland 'It is impossible with every wish to keep him in good humour...you will arrange to keep him in good temper.' Radcliffe had to be humoured because he could be used, but he was not respected by the military, and Maitland so disliked him he obstructed his long-expected baronetcy. The military also had little respect for other members of the community who were supposed to be supporting them - the Special Constables. Several complaints were made about them not turning up for guard duty, or, on at least one occasion for insisiting on joining a patrol when the commander didn't want them along. The Huddersfield deputy constable, George Whitehead, was also resented. Maitland described him to Acland as 'insufferable in point of money... If he comes to you again, send him off, for I will not keep him any longer.' [32]

Perhaps underlying Maitlands disdain for the civil authorities was distaste at the role the military was being called on to play. Huddersfield, a small but growing manufacturing town, and its surrounding villages, were under virtual military occupation and near martial law. British troops were being employed to dominate and intimidate British subjects in order to force through technological and economic change. The government must have viewed the situation around Huddersfield as extremely alarming to have committed so many regular troops to put down a rising amongst the English when they were desperately needed on the continent to fight the French. They may have had good reason for concern. A former Mirfield man, Richard Milnes, a decade or so later, recorded the popular belief that 'If Bonaparte had invaded England...[oppression] had provoked the people of England to such an extreme of desperation that they would have joined Bonaparte.' Little wonder, so soon after 1798 when French troops had landed and fought alongside Irish rebels against the British, that the government took seriously Luddite threats that they would be joined 'by the French and the Papists in Ireland.' The assassination of Perceval on 11 May caused great alarm. A friend of Radcliffe wrote from London expressing the relief felt in ruling circles that there was no political motive - 'it was at best fortunate that Bellingham was neither a Papist, an Irishman, nor a petitioner for the repeal of the Orders in Council, nor a reformer of parliament.' [33]

Such fears turned Huddersfield into a garrison town. Troops and militia were brought in in large numbers to form an army of occupation in hostile territory. By late June there were 98 men of the 2nd Dragoons and 300 of the Cumberland Militia in Huddersfield. Three months later the number of troops in the town had risen to 1000, some brought from considerable distances - Stirlingshire, South Devon and Kent. There must have been major problems of communication between them and the native Yorkshire folk, allowing for the fact that at this period regional accents were far stronger and may well have rendered various elements unintelligible to each other. This aspect alone can not have endeared the soldiers to the local population.

Most were billetted on the 33 pubs in the town, and the *Mercury* acknowledged 'Publicans are very much distressed to accommodate them.' Since landlords were required by law to provide straw, candles, food and drink, but were rarely paid sufficient to cover costs, this is not suprising. Housing soldiers could impoverish the host. Because of the general animosity in the neighbourhood and the need to keep soldiers together for their own protection, less use was made of private houses, yet there were still complaints that householders had been called from their beds in the early hours and forced to accommodate troops. Even some of the more 'well-disposed' might have felt they were better off being left to the mercies of the Luddites than thus protected.

John Littlewood, adjutant in the local Agbrigg Militia, experienced 'a great deal of trouble in fitting small houses in many of the villages for the reception of small parties of infantry,' and was offended that his efforts went unrecognised when he was passed over for appointment as Master of the new barracks. Some soldiers of the South Devon Militia and 2nd Dragoons were accompanied by wives and, in the early months of 1813, there were at least nine children baptised at Huddersfield parish church, four of them on 24 January. Most of these women would have found lodgings, though a few might have been allowed into the primitive accommodation of the guard house or barracks, and the combined picture of troops, wives and children suggests a town bursting at the seams with an unaccustomed, and largely unwelcome, influx of population.

The *Mercury* of 4 April reported that 'Leeds and Huddersfield have, with their piquets, military patrols etc. assumed more the appearance of garrison towns than the peaceful abodes of trade and industry!' Not only Huddersfield but also its surrounding villages were occupied by troops, and there were guard-posts at Holmfirth, Lockwood, Almondbury and Marsden. In 1864 it was recollected that at Marsden, home of both the hated Horsfall and of the Taylor Brothers, manufacturers of the cropping frames, the 10th King's Bays, the 15th Hussars and the Scotch Greys were stationed at different times, but moved around regularly 'lest they should become indoctrinated with the seditious opinions of the Luddites... Men then, and still living, declare that these soldiers when off-duty were dissipated and licentious, and a terror to the peacably disposed; and that they exercised a present, and left a lasting influence for evil upon the morals and manners of the people.' It was also remembered in Marsden that 'no lights were permitted in any dwellings after 9 o'clock,' whilst, in Honley, recollections of the curfew survived for a century. It is clear that anyone found walking abroad at night was liable to be arrested and questioned, causing great inconvenience to many honest people going about their lawful business, but the troops never seem to have troubled the Luddites themselves who knew only too well how to evade the patrols under the cover of darkness.[34]

A further imposition of the military was arms collecting - both to disarm potential Luddites and to secure weapons from theft. Understandably, this was not popular with those who felt they needed them for their own protection. Major Gordon's men had collected 200 stand of arms by the beginning of May, and the weapons, belonging to 24 manufacturers and other respectable inhabitants, most of them from the Holme Valley, were stored in the depot of the Militia until 7 August. John Littlewood, the militia adjutant, was then ordered by the magistrates to secure them in 'the Storeroom at the back of George Wilson's house in King's street.' A mini arsenal of 'Ten cases of arms, number in each case unknown,' along with 260 muskets, 47 pistols, 17 swords, 4 blunderbusses and 3 bayonets were moved to King Street - which may explain the presence of a ruin, an 'architectural oddity,' reputed to be a fort, still extant in the 1930s.[35]

As well as the military, Special Constables were enrolled from among the better-off inhabitants to maintain 'Watch and Ward' and carry out patrols and sometimes searches. The 'Watch and Ward Act', which conscripted residents for duty, was unpopular in Huddersfield and 'considerable difficulties' obstructed its effective implementation, the *Mercury* suggesting a voluntary scheme would be better received. West Riding magistrates backed a plan to set up Associations 'for the preservation of the Public Peace' in each township, but this also met with mixed success. Huddersfield had such an Association in July, with 160 men organised into 8 'classes' of 20 to reinforce 31 Specials. Holmfirth and its surrounding hamlets had the largest body of Specials, 76 men and a further 109 'ready to be sworn'. By early September they were carrying out nightly patrols alongside the military. Thirty Specials had been enrolled under 'Watch and Ward' in Marsden in July, but in contrast, in Honley there were only 9, 'but none come forward to watch and ward'. The situation in Honley had changed by September when there were 57 Specials, an Association and Watch and Ward duties being carried out every night. The Specials seem to have been as unpopular as were the military. When a Huddersfield stable belonging to the Special, Allen Edwards, was set on fire on 27 April, it was said to be because he had made himself 'obnoxious...by the vigilant discharge of his duty.' Often drawn from the ranks of major employers and professional men, the Specials polarised the community on clear class lines. [36]

The combination of curfews, arms searches, questioning, 'taking up' on suspicion and the general atmosphere of fear must have been a totally novel experience for most people. Add this to the frequent lights, signal rockets, flares and signal shots, used by the Luddites to distract the soldiers from the targets of their raids and the nightly apprehension of the raids themselves, and the area presents itself as an exciting, if not comfortable, place to live. Yet, for all their activity, the military seem to have been singularly unsuccesful - possibly because mounted soldiers were too noisy and cumbersome to be useful in counter-guerilla warfare, particularly when, as in the attack on Vickerman's, the soldiers and their mounts were in widely separate places when the alarm was given. Both when Rawfolds was attacked and Horsfall shot, it took troops an unreasonably long time to reach the scene. It would seem that, faced with the general hostility of the people, their clattering around was of no avail. The soldiers probably hated the posting as much as those on whom they were imposed disliked their presence. Without doubt, most of them lived under harsh, unpleasant and overcrowded conditions, in addition to having to endure the open hostility of the locals.

If the conditions of the soldiers' daily lives were harsh it would seem that those of their prisoners were worse. We have a clear picture of the disgusting conditions of the Huddersfield 'Towser' when local insurgents were held there five years later and there is no reason to imagine that they were any better in 1812. They may even have been worse. On 13 September Acland reported that, due to the number of prisoners, he had had to divide them between the Towser and the main guardroom, because the former was 'very small and confined'. He also mentioned that 'subsistence' was required, 'In some instances it appears to have been altogether forgotten or neglected.' On 9 December he asked Radcliffe if he would allow the prisoners in the Towser to sleep in the guardroom 'as the nights are very cold...the condition where they are must be very miserable.' Some sympathy at least from the officer whose efforts had put them there. The attention of the Home Office was also brought to the 'bad conditions of Huddersfield gaol'. [37]

'Luddite' has become a name synonymous with violence directed against progress by mindless machine breakers, who tried to prevent improvements in trade, men who were described by Lord Fitzwilliam, in a strikingly modern cliche, as 'murderers and terrorists.' A closer look at the actual events of 1812/13 shows a rather different picture, and reveals that, when it came to violence, the government, magistrates and others in authority proved themselves rather more bloodthirsty and violent than their working class victims. The score of deaths in Yorkshire alone would read Government 19, Luddites 1. Because it was done in the name of law, the violence of the authorities is seldom seen as such, but violence it was.

Due to the activities of the Nottinghamshire Luddites in 1811, none of whom suffered the death penalty at the subsequent trials held under Judge Bailey, the Perceval government decided that, from here on, the sentence for machine breaking would be death. Accordingly a Bill was introduced into the House, and proceded to the House of Lords, where it became the subject of the maiden speech of Lord Byron who thundered, 'Are there not capital punishments sufficient in your statutes ? Is there not blood enough upon your penal code...Will you erect a gibbet in every field and hang up men like scarecrows ?' Not content with adding yet another capital offence to what has been described as 'Europe's most barbarous criminal code,' the government then sought to bring in a further death penalty for administering an illegal oath. Secretary Ryder introduced the Bill on 5 May, which became law, despite the MP Samuel Whitbread pointing out the anomaly that 'No distinction was made between the crime of taking an unlawful oath and the assassination of a man.' By the time Luddite activities commenced in this area the death penalty applied to frame-breaking and, soon after, to the administration, or taking, of illegal oaths. Beginning to demolish a mill, and even blacking one's face as a disguise were also capital crimes, making most Luddite activities punishable by hanging. Murder was only one of the many crimes for which a man risked his neck and so it seems strange that murder was not resorted to more often. A man could only hang once - and why not for a sheep as a lamb? Yet violence against the person was not a hallmark of the Luddites. Only one man died at their hands, and although many were shot at, these can be seen as warnings, rather than serious assassination attempts. Seventeen men were hanged at York for their 'crimes' yet had the Luddites gone in for mass murder the sentences could not have been much more severe. Rather than indulging in gratuitous violence, the Luddites seem to have gone out of their way to perpetrate as little violence as possible in the majority of cases in which they were involved. The attacks on cropping shops had one purpose only, the destruction of the cropping frames and hand-shears, thereby ensuring that those who had installed machinery could not immediately set up business again. The only items stolen were guns and money, to further their cause. On many occasions the attackers asked for the keys to the workshops to avoid unnecessary damage and often behaved with great politeness, wishing their victims 'good night' on departing. In the light of this, the attack on Vickerman's mill stands out yet more clearly as one where a strong personal hatred of the man led to uncharacteristic vandalism .[38]

What then of the one undoubted act of extreme violence perpetrated by the Luddites - the murder of Horsfall ? Several factors undoubtedly influenced this decision to 'leave the machines and turn on the masters.' At Rawfolds, blood had been shed - Luddite blood. The masters had been the first to use violence against the person. Two Luddites were dead, it was strongly rumoured that a further two died of their wounds later, and many of the Luddites were injured to a greater or lesser degree. Cartwright himself said 'Many are certainly wounded, the traces of blood being very heavy in different directions.' There seems to have been a feeling amongst the Luddites that, now the masters had broken the rules, they themselves would turn to a new means of attack. Ben Walker claimed as much in his deposition - 'I think if no one had been shot we should never have thought of taking anybody's life'. Clearly, the deaths of at least two of their close knit band of men deeply affected them. Rawfolds also highlighted the lengths to which the masters were prepared to go to protect their cropping machines. Cartwright had installed vicious spiked rollers on the stairs and had a tub of vitriol ready to pour down on any who gained entry. The *Mercury* remarked 'The assailants have much reason to rejoice that they did not succeed in entering - had they affected an entrance the deaths of vast numbers of them from a raking fire which they could neither have returned nor controlled, would have been inevitable.' An additional feature at Arthur Hirst's Woodbottom Mill, Marsden, was an ingenious trap-door over the water wheel, which would certainly have killed any attackers breaking in, possibly causing even greater loss of life than at Rawfolds.

The masters, then, showed little regard for human life in protecting their machines and all were prepared to shoot to kill in the war between masters and men. The larger mills had become fortresses and, after the Rawfolds fight, the futility of attacking them was apparent to the croppers. They had used every means in their power to persuade the masters to remove the obnoxious machinery, and some had died in the process. Their next move was to be against the masters themselves - and Horsfall's assassination was the inevitable result of this new way of thinking. 'Vengeance for the blood of the innocent' had been their cry after the defeat at Rawfolds, and Horsfall paid for their blood with his own. It was a dramatic act, and, as with any death brought about by a politically motivated group, it was seen by some at the time, and perhaps by more since, as the one act which deprived the Luddites of the right to any sympathy and understanding. The taking of one life is seen by many as far more reprehensible than the judicial taking of seventeen in reprisal. But the Luddites themselves did not see it in this light, and did not regard themselves as murderers, or indeed, criminals. After the hangings, Colonel Norton reported of the executed men 'I really believe they did not consider it *any great* if *any offence*....They either felt themselves bound by *some oath* not to acknowledge their crime or were *insensible* to it. [They] died praying most loudly, but I do not think at all repenting *the* Crime...I do not believe any of them had a proper sense of the Crime they died for, I mean any of the eight I call Luddites.' [39]

January 1813 saw the culmination of official violence. Seventeen men were hanged - of which only three died for alleged murder. Seven were transported - and several of these would have been executed instead, if their 'crime' of administering an illegal oath had been committed *after* it became a capital offence. Baines himself escaped death by only two days. All the men held at York faced a potential death sentence, and only public disgust at the wholesale slaughter prevented more from being hanged. Byron's prediction had been correct - in order to ensure that terror was instilled into any of the workers remaining free who might be inclined to continue the Luddite struggle - they had indeed found 'twelve butchers for a jury, and a Jefferies for a judge.'

As early as 16 May preparations were afoot for the trials at York to be held at public expense, although there had, as yet, been few arrests. At the end of October, Fitzwilliam emphasised the urgency for trials 'Examples of detection, conviction and punishment can alone avert the evils of further Lud outbreaks during the dark winter nights, and this is not possible if the trials are put off till spring.' Further delay, he reiterated a few days later, would make the Luddites continue to appear invulnerable and 'might mean some of the evidence may be taken off.' [40]

Balanced against the pressure to hold trials as quickly as possible was the consideration that they had to guarantee convictions. Maitland was concerned that acquittals would be 'a triumph for the disaffected' and law officers held the opinion that, with only the evidence of accomplices and in the absence of confirmatory evidence, it was better to postpone the trials rather than risk an acquittal. Radcliffe himself was confident by the end of October that it was 'likely that all those committed would be convicted.' Maitland, however, was worried that the magistrates' 'overzeal unless it be corrected... may lead to numerous acquittals which I think your lordship will agree with me is a thing extremely to be avoided.' He also advised Sidmouth that 'if we make good our cases...and do not attempt too much, I think the spirit of the late combinations will be completely broken.'[41]

Both Maitland and the judiciary displayed more awareness than Radcliffe or Lloyd of the need for caution if they were not to lose the already limited public sympathy and credulity in the face of suspect prosecution evidence. This was reflected at the end of Schofield's trial, when the prosecution counsel announced that charges against some other prisoners would be dropped, ostensibly in the interests of leniency and mercy, but the real reason was explained by one of the prosecution solicitors 'The effect of this step is to release about six prisoners without prosecution, against whom the evidence is next to nothing.'[42]

Similar 'leniency and mercy' was shown to other prisoners in cases which Justice Park prevented from being brought to trial 'from a desire not to have the witnesses who had given evidence, particularly the accomplices...again submitted unnecessarily to public inspection.' He was also concerned that some of the cases fell within the Riot Act 'and how far rioters might go in the execution of their plans without incurring the guilt of felony. It did not appear to me wise to have this too generally known, especially in the County of York.' Could it be that some of the 'capital offences' would not bear scrutiny ? Park further advised that the government should pay the compensation claimed for wrongful arrest, rather than proceed with resumed trials. Yet another admission that most of the cases would not hold water, and reflecting some doubt on the 'safe convictions' of some of those hanged. [43]

That some of the evidence was dubious is not suprising, given the even more dubious means of obtaining it. Radcliffe's comparatively humane method of investigation was to have suspects 'taken up' and brought into Milnsbridge House for questioning, often on several occasions. Dilapidated shell of a building it may be today, but it has the historical significance of, at one time or another, holding within its walls many local Luddites and their supporters. Though his methods might have irritated the innocent and frightened the guilty, they were innocuous in comparison with those of Lloyd, whose forays into Yorkshire so much annoyed Radcliffe. Lloyd preferred to hold suspects in close and unpleasant custody, using fear and threats to force information and confessions out of them. Was what he heard what he wanted to hear, or was it the truth? Perhaps by the time he had finished with them some of his victims were prepared to confess to anything or name anyone. The fantastic plot revealed by Barrowclough under interrogation, involving a planned rising helped by the French, showed the extremes to which some susceptible detainees could go to ingratiate themselves with their interrogators. Even non-Luddites were not spared his unpleasant grilling, as the wounded Hinchliffe discovered when he was encouraged by Lloyd to suddenly remember that Schofield was one of the men who shot him. Lloyd admitted that some physical abuse went on and, although darker rumours of torture were not substantiated, those in his custody, even by the standards of the day, suffered inhuman and degrading treatment. Maitland, assessing Lloyd's investigations, thought that 'There is no doubt much of it is out of the strict letter of the law, though, I believe, perfectly in the spirit both of the law and of the constitution.' [44].

The anxiety of the authorities to obtain convictions and exemplary sentences is evident in the desire of all concerned to exclude Judge Bailey from any proceedings. He had presided over the previous Luddite trials, where, much to the annoyance of Radcliffe, he had 'done much harm' by not hanging anyone. Radcliffe did not want his own work undoing and requested the Home Office 'But pray exclude Judge Bailey from the Commission. His decisions at the last assize give great encouragement to the Ludds who call him their friend'. Acland too thought there was enough evidence to convict George Mellor 'if tried by any Judge but Bailey.' Establishing a Special Commission under a reliable judge, more akin to a Jeffries than a Bailey, was seen as further insurance against acquittals or lenient sentences, and Radcliffe did not conceal his satisfaction, 'I am very glad to hear there is no chance of the prisoners being tried by Judge Bailey.' [45]

The most macabre evidence that the authorities now regarded the results of the Horsfall murder trial as a foregone conclusion, and that deterrence was more important than justice, is apparent in the ghoulish discussions about where the accused should be executed and the fate of their corpses. Even before the trial had opened Hobhouse announced 'I lay gibbeting out of the question. The alternative is ordering the bodies to be anatomised. But is there any surgeon at or near Huddersfield who would dare to dissect the bodies? If not I am very much disposed to think that an execution at York should be preferred.' Acland, writing from Huddersfield, suggested that the murderers should be executed on the spot where the crime was committed. 'I conceive the bodies may be consigned to the infirmary at Leeds for dissection and will be most acceptable to the medical practitioners there. It is also very possible here may easily be found the work for that purpose, but I think that no resident surgeon could be found to undertake it.' On reflection the authorities decided that, rather than instilling fear, they would create an explosive situation if they attempted to hang the three men in Huddersfield or return their bodies for anything other than a decent Christian burial. The funerals of the Rawfolds victims and of those returned from York in January, showed how the majority of the population regarded the Luddites as martyrs. To have strung up Mellor, Thorpe and Smith in the town and then carted their bodies off to be hacked up by some local surgeon would, potentially, have sparked off the very disturbances the trials were intended to deter.

In view of the pressure on the authorities to make arrests and obtain convictions, whether real evidence was forthcoming or not, it is hardly suprising that the conduct of the trials themselves does not bear close scrutiny and scarcely conforms to the much vaunted idea of 'British justice'! Even an unprejudiced jury can be led by clever barristers and false evidence to come to the desired conclusions, and, in this case, the political background of the trials made the jury far from unprejudiced. Rede, writing his *History of York Castle* in the late 1820s, described the significance of the possible miscarriage of justice in terms still relevant to historical, or legal, inquiry today.

> **'It is apparently useless to find fault with the verdicts pronounced long since, and the penalties of which have been inflicted and endured years ago; but if we were to be deterred from investigating truth because it is too late to prevent the infliction of punishment we might close our labours at once. The exposition of the errors of other days become warnings for the future.'**

Cases in recent years have shown that verdicts made by juries acting in good faith and within the requirements of the legal system can be overturned as 'unsafe'. Old injustices are as unjust as recent ones, and if safe verdicts can not be guaranteed in our own time, how much less likely they were in 1813 when no investigative journalist was likely to be interested in exonerating a working class 'criminal'. This is not to say that none of those convicted were guilty - most of them were probably guilty of some 'crime' which was a capital offence at the time, but, with a fair trial, some may have been acquitted of the crime with which they were actually charged, or received a more lenient sentence.[46]

In particular the conduct of the prosecuting counsel, Mr Park, is open to serious criticism. During his opening speeches he was adept at putting words into the mouths of witnesses who, under cross-examination, failed to come up with the statements attributed to them. This happened on several occasions and was condemned by Rede as 'an illiberal and unjust practice, and should be exploded, *more especially as counsel are not allowed to do the same on the part of the prisoners.*' But once something was stated the jury could not be expected to forget it. Jonathan Dean, after his arrest for the Rawfolds affair, made a voluntary confession on the understanding that to do so would be to his advantage. Park read it out, but when the circumstances of the confession were questioned, he agreed to withdraw it from evidence. By then the damage was done, and the words planted in the minds of the jurors. Park also attempted to discredit defence witnesses by implying they made a virtue out of committing perjury, 'Their maxim is...that it is no harm to tell one lie to save a brother.' If systematic perjury was taking place then it would have been the duty of the court to indict the perjurors, and that did not occur. Justice Le Blanc was less explicit in his suggestions of perjury, but he made great play on the fallibility of memory. 'This must depend very much, not only on the credit given to those different witnesses who have been called, but certainly, at this distance of time, upon the accuracy of their recollection; and some of them, you will see clearly, according to the account given by other witnesses, must be mistaken as to time.' His assumption was that witnesses for the defence had unreliable clocks and memories, but that those of the prosecution were reliable. Apart from his seeming obsession with faulty clocks, he made much of the length of time between events and trials, especially in the case of the Horsfall shooting. Witnesses were

> 'speaking of a transaction which not only took place a long time ago, but was not imputed to the prisoners at the bar till a considerable time after it had taken place...Nothing happened immediately after the transaction to lead these persons particularly to watch so as to be accurate in the hour or time upon that particular evening, when they saw these persons at a particular place...'

His assessment was that it was unlikely that people could remember, after the lapse of over eight months, the exact time of such banal minutiae as selling a watch or paying a bill. But this is to underrate the impact of both the Rawfolds attack and Horsfall's shooting. Huddersfield was a very small town where news travelled fast, and such outstanding local events, in a memorable year like 1812, would have imprinted themselves firmly in the minds of all. In the same way people recollect, many years after the event, minor details of where they were and what they were doing when they heard that Kennedy was shot. During the Rawfolds trials several of the witnesses specifically mention that they could pin their memories to the fact that it was 'the night of the Rawfolds stir.' and this must also be true of Horsfall's death.

The majority of the defence evidence consisted of alibis. It is difficult to see how this could be otherwise, when the only defence of those accused of being at a particular place at a specific time was to prove that they were somewhere else. Many of the alibis were quite convincing and, in particular, that of George Mellor bears scrutiny. But the prosecution, judge and jury appear to have had an inconsistent attitude to alibis. Some were believed, some were not, even when the same witnesses were speaking in different cases, as if they gave reliable evidence one day and were lying the next. The most contradictory example of this was in the case of Joseph Brook, when the jury found him not guilty - but then went on to say they did not believe one word of his alibi. Park also cast aspersions on this type of evidence, remarking that they often had an authentic ring because 'the circumstances generally are true: only give another date and then the story is all true.'

Little wonder that the jury became confused, in the absence of any defence counter argument to balance misdirection from the prosecution and judge. This was not confined to the Luddite trials but was a feature of the judicial system - the accused could not speak for themselves and their counsel could not make out a case or address the jury. Their efforts were confined to examining their own witnesses and the cross-examination of the prosecution's, and for the Luddites this had the drawback that their counsel, the celebrated radical Brougham, was conspicuous by his inaction, and left them out on a limb. Perhaps he, like other leading middle class radicals, feared being identified too closely with a band of working class subversives. Defending Queen Caroline seven years later was a far better career move.

Another flaw in the trials is the rather cavalier attitude towards any positive identification of the accused. Martha Mellor definitely identified George, but even at the trial seemed unsure whether or not the other man was Thorpe. There was a good deal of 'did not positively know but thought...' in the evidence of witnesses from Joseph Mellor's household. Parr, the eyewitness to the murder 'did not know the young men in the dock,' and Mrs Robinson, landlady of the Coach & Horses at Honley, was never asked whether or not she recognised Smith and Walker. At no point did any prosecution witness point the finger and say 'that was the man.' Names were given only by the informers, whose credibility must be in doubt, since they were intent on saving their own necks. Some efforts at identification were made at the Rawfolds trial - Hall was asked to point out the men in the dock whom he had seen there. But again, this was used against defence witnesses. Abraham Berry was prevented from completing his account of James Haigh's alibi when he was unable to make a positive identification of William Hall, after saying he believed he was there at the same time. He was told that consequently it could not be received as evidence, in contrast to the tolerant attitude shown to the prosecution's unsubstantiated claims.

Perhaps the final injustice of the trials was the unseemly haste with which Mellor, Thorpe and Smith were sent to the gallows. Only 36 hours elapsed between their convictions and the executions. This certainly left no opportunity to lodge an appeal had they been so inclined. In view of the advance preparation for their disposal this is perhaps not suprising, but the three were dead before any of those with whom they were jointly accused of other offences had even stood trial.

Maitland expressed satisfaction with the outcome of the Special Commission which had 'succeeded in every point beyond my most sanguine expectations' and, presumably acting on the General's advice, Beckett, from the Home Office, informed Radcliffe on 20 January that 'to test the impression made by the York trials' it was intended to withdraw the troops from the area. Radcliffe, much to his annoyance, was asked to cease the pursuit of the Luddites. Despite the retribution exacted by the trials he did not think all the guilty had been brought to justice. Nor did he believe that it signalled the danger was over - a fear which seemed confirmed by a shot fired into Milnsbridge House on 20 January. [47]

The government's repression of the Luddite rising was founded on dubious irregularities and blatant injustices. Caught up in the machinations of the state there was never any hope of escape for those whom authority had decided should be made an example of for the terrorising of others. The trials displayed many inconsistences and contradictory evidence - not just between witnesses for defence and prosecution, but between the prosecution witnesses themselves. This emphasises a rather murky area of Luddite history, of numerous suspects, seemingly arbitrary arrests and releases, unexplained statements, lies or half truths, which make the events of 1812 'a riddle within an enigma.'

Numerous people, suspected of being active Luddites or staunch supporters, were never questioned or arrested. Vickerman and 'A Friend to Peace' named several strong suspects, while Radcliffe certainly believed that Thomas Brook, hanged for his part in the Rawfolds attack, was 'Chief Lud' of the area, contradicting the idea later put by the prosecution at the trials, that the ringleader was George Mellor. In particular, there were several suspects for the Horsfall assassination before the final four were fixed on. There seems to have been no shortage of men prepared to boast that they had been involved in the shooting. Lloyd noted that 'the Luddites so much rejoiced at it that they were proud to be considered connected with the most principal leaders.' One such was Richard Tattersall who, whilst held in the Manchester New Bayley, claimed to have been present when Horsfall was shot. According to the *Mercury* of 10 October, Joshua Haigh, a soldier, was committed to York on his own admission of the Horsfall murder. A private in the 51st Regiment of Foot, he was arrested as a deserter in Dublin - yet, since he was already under arrest when the shooting happened, he could not possibly have been involved. Despite this, on

24 September, two women deposed that a Joshua Haigh had claimed he was one of the four and as late as 8 October Ben Walker's mother gave evidence against him. A Joshua Haigh, described as a cloth dresser, was detained at York but was discharged without prosecution, accused only of the attack on Rawfolds. If this was the same Joshua, he may have gone on the run after the attack and enlisted to help his escape. There seems to have been some confusion between Joshua, James Haigh of Dalton, and Samuel Haigh of Totties, who was sent to York under strong guard on 1 August, accused by the highly imaginative Barrowclough of the Horsfall shooting. Yet Samuel too was eventually indicted only for burglary and arms stealing and then discharged. James Varley was also almost charged with the Horsfall murder, but only because he seemed to be deeply involved in the cover up, showing how this accusation was used to intimidate those known to be innocent of it. He was also eventually indicted only with burglary and arms stealing, then discharged and not used to give evidence. [48]

One of the most unlikely suspects of the murder was Joseph Mellor himself, taken with Thomas Smith and Benjamin Armitage on 11 October, though he was already on Radcliffe's list of Luddite suspects. Just what, if anything, was Joseph Mellor's involvement with Luddism? As George Mellor's cousin he might well have been deeply implicated. It was his evidence which sent George to York Castle, yet his statement was made when he himself was a suspect. Subpoenaed as a prosecution witness, he gave evidence which contradicted himself and his wife and did not match his original statement. For example, as to the pistols supposedly left at his house, his first statement was that Varley came to collect them in the early hours of the following day. He then altered this to the following Sunday, but the Judge, summing up, said that a week after Joseph had told Varley he had the pistols, they were gone, with no account of who had fetched them. [49]

Joseph also said that he arrived home at seven that evening, and that he had heard of the shooting on his way home. His wife said she did not learn of it until after eight, when people called in with the news. Why did Joseph not tell her before that - and why did it take him an hour to travel from Huddersfield to Lockwood ? Even Martha's statement that the two men arrived at a quarter past six would be too early for them to have fled from the plantation after the shooting. There certainly seems to have been some confusion as to time in the household. Durrance, one of the apprentices, said Joseph arrived home one and a half hours after George left, which, according to Martha was at half past six, meaning that either Joseph arrived home at eight or that in fact George's departure was at half past five. This would corroborate George's own account, in which he admitted being at Joseph's house that day, along with another man, but had left an hour earlier than claimed by Martha. Even more strange would have been George's decision to flee to his cousin's house, knowing that one of Joseph's apprentices was the nephew and namesake of Francis Vickerman of Taylor Hill, an arch-enemy of the Luddites. Mary Dyson, Joseph's servant girl, was also niece of Clement Dyson, whose cropping shop, which shared the same building at Dungeon as Joseph's, had been subjected to two Luddite attacks. Joseph's premises hardly seem to have been a safe house for Luddites, especially recognisable ones, on the run.

One intriguing aspect of Mary Dyson and her testimony (she was never called as witness) is the fact that she seems to have disappeared only a few days after making her statement on the 18 October. The magistrate John Walker, of Lascelles Hall, an owner of Dungeon Mill and therefore presumably acquainted with events in the neighbourhood, questioned Joseph on why he had dismissed her, since she was obviously a valuable witness, and why he himself had been away from home for several days - behaviour he thought 'imprudent', if not suspect. Joseph explained that he had been visiting relatives and that the girl had not been dismissed but had been taken away by a constable. If the magistrates, Walker, and especially, Radcliffe, knew nothing of this, then on whose orders was she taken away, why and to where? One of Joseph's apprentices seems to have suffered a similar fate. Walker advised that 'the witness Oldham should be removed as soon as possible,' yet, by the time of the trials, he too had disappeared. Martha Mellor said in court that he had left because of misbehaviour, after George Mellor was committed to York. She then stated that he had run away and she did not know where he was, or in the words of the judge, he had 'absconded'. Neither his importance nor his disappearance were ever explained.[50]

Another intriguing aspect of the witnesses from Joseph Mellor's household is the repeated affirmation by George Mellor that they should tell the truth about the day of the shooting. If their evidence could condemn him, why should he insist on this? George's letter to Thomas Ellis, smuggled out of York Castle, reiterates the point that he believed that the original testimonies of Joseph's household sustained his alibi:

> **'Please to give my respect to my cousin and tell him to stick fast to what he swore the first time before Radcliffe and I hope his wife will do the same, that I left their house before 5pm and I did not leave anything at their house and if the boy swears anything tell my cousin to contradict him and say he told him a different story that there had been a man had left them and he did not know him and as for the girl she cannot swear anything I know that will harm me and tell the boys to stick by what they said the first time. If not they are proved foresworn... Remember a soul is of more value than work or gold.'**

Whether Joseph received this message is not known, but Ellis was suspected of giving him an even clearer one by shooting at him just before his appearance as a prosecution witness. On his return from the trials he found cloth on his tenters chalked with 'BFBSGL' - Blood For Blood Says General Ludd. Interestingly, William Cartwright believed that Joseph had done this himself, possibly to divert lingering suspicion about his own involvement in Luddism. One final curious association of Joseph with Luddism is mentioned by Ahier in his *Legends and Traditions of Huddersfield* who recorded that when a disused building was demolished at Dungeon a cache of old firearms was found in a chimney. He believes that these were part of the preparations to defend Dungeon Mill in 1812, but storing arms in a chimney stack indicates more of a desire to keep them hidden than have them ready for defence. There may have been more to Joseph Mellor than meets the eye. [51]

What of the chief prosecution witness, Benjamin Walker? In court he told one blatant lie, which can be proved as such, when he swore that he sent his mother to give evidence to Radcliffe about the Horsfall shooting. The truth was very different. She had, in fact, been taken into custody on the orders of Lloyd, who said of her 'I have run away with one of the witnesses to prevent her being tampered with and have placed her in my own house where she will more fully and freely give her examination.' However, Mrs Walker held out against Lloyd's methods, even when told (in the middle of the night!) that her son had been arrested. She did however accuse Thorpe of being one of the four murderers, and he was consequently examined on 19 October, though released again. Ben Walker had indeed been arrested, again on the advice of Lloyd. He had already been questioned along with George Mellor on 12 October, denying everything. He was arrested on 17 October and held at Milnsbridge House but, despite being subjected to Lloyd's interrogation methods, it was reported on 20 October that 'Benjamin Walker has been examined but nothing has come out.' But within twenty four hours Walker had cracked, and it was announced the following day that Walker 'this evening confessed he was one of the four' along with Mellor, Thorpe and Smith. However, his confession was not quite polished enough, for he stated that Mellor fired two shots, Thorpe one and either he or Smith also fired. To be unsure of whether or not he had fired a shot which may have killed a man seems a curious lapse of memory. By 22 October he had made a more satisfactory statement - only Mellor and Thorpe had fired. This statement sent Thorpe and Smith to join Mellor in York Castle, and himself to safe custody in the House of Correction. Walker had been offered indemnity - as an active Luddite involved in all forms of capital offence he would have hanged - and the possibility of the £2,000 reward. He had been held in close and possibly brutal confinement and subjected to constant interrogation. Was it a combination of these factors which caused him to turn informer ? Did he confess the truth, or make a statement which would satisfy his interrogators, or fabricate a story for the sake of his own skin and the possibility of financial reward? There was plenty of time between his statement and the trials to polish a story, embellish it with details obtained from others, and synchronise it with those of other eager informants such as William Hall. There is always the possibility that neither Walker nor the other three shot Horsfall, or that one or more of them were involved along with others never accused. Did he confine his lies to the one about his mother, or, by the end of his interrogations was he prepared to swear to anything ? [52]

Without doubt, one of his statements about the shooting directly contradicts the evidence of the eyewitness, Parr, who was adamant that he saw four men together at the corner of the plantation when the shots were fired, that he had seen four men in the plantation before Horsfall drew close, but that once he had reached it, one man stooped and fired whilst the other three were standing beside him. The *Mercury* report of 2 May specifically mentioned 'four men, each armed with a horse pistol, appeared in a small plantation and placed the barrel of their pistols in apertures in the wall, apparently prepared for the purpose; the muzzle of two of these pieces Mr Horsfall distinctly saw...they all four fired.' Horsfall, in his deathbed deposition before magistrate Scott mentioned seeing four men. Yet despite this, Walker insisted that Smith and himself had been quite hidden and crouched down at the back of the plantation where they could not be seen, and at no time were the four of them together in the corner of the plantation. Horsfall suffered at least four separate wounds and it seems impossible that only one or two fired.

Nor could Walker agree with the other chief prosecution witness, William Hall, when it came to his own examination before Radcliffe. Walker claimed, that when he was first taken up, he asked Hall to provide an alibi. Hall denied that he had ever done so, or that he had told Joseph Rushworth that he had cleared Walker, by showing he could not have been at the plantation at the time of the shooting. Rushworth, however, confirmed that he had been told this by Hall on 12 October. Walker's father was the centre of further confusion. The prosecution claimed that, after the shooting, Mellor swore him to secrecy on the assumption that he had heard the story from Ben, but, in fact, Mellor's confession was the first he had heard of it. Yet Ben asserted that, on the night of the shooting, he had told both his parents details of the event. It should not be forgotten that Walker himself was given alibis for the time of the murder - alibis which he certainly did not want or need. Mary Thorpe, Wood's servant, said that both he and Smith came to their 'drinking' at six o'clock, whilst Wood's apprentice, John Bower, claimed that Smith and Walker were hardening the press at some time shortly after the news of the shooting came at seven. William Hirst, Wood's lodger, swore that he met Walker in the yard at that time and, just having heard about Horsfall, told Walker, who replied 'That is too good news to be true.'

Walker presented a pathetic sight after the hangings, 'pale ghastly and hardly able to stand', in strong contrast to his former comrades who had just died with such courage and resolution. When, in March, the Quakers Joseph Wood and Thomas Shillitoe visited him he was not only still 'pale and ghastly' and unsteady on his feet, but also exhibited 'such apparent self condemnation in his countenance, we thought we had not before witnessed, as if he felt himself an outcast...his mind appeared much agitated...' Was it just that he felt himself an outcast, or did his conscience trouble him for having sent former friends, guilty or otherwise, to the gallows? [53]

Walker is perhaps partly absolved by an unexplained report in the *Mercury* of 24 October which states that when George Mellor was arrested he behaved with the greatest effrontery until, faced with the informer, he changed colour and gasped for breath. Leaving the room after hearing the informer's evidence he swore 'Damn that man, he has done for me.' It has always been assumed that the informer was Ben Walker, but this was not possible. The dates simply do not fit - Mellor was committed to York between 10 and 16 October. Walker was not arrested until the 17 and made no kind of confession at all until 21 October, so he would hardly have been in a position to confront Mellor in Milnsbridge House. Was the informer Joseph Mellor, Kinder, Durrance, Vickerman Jnr, or someone else entirely? This mystery may never be answered, but at least it exonerates Benjamin Walker of the crime of which history and tradition have accused him - that he was the first man to turn informer for the money. Judas he may have become, but it was not his original intent. It may also explain why he was eventually refused the promised reward on the grounds that he was not the first to come forward. Who, if anyone, did receive the blood-money?

Another twist to the Horsfall case is the anonymous letter from 'V', apparently Vickerman, who appears to have detailed knowledge about the shooting. He states that four men were involved, two of whom had visited Joseph Mellor's, changed their clothes and then gone away for about an hour before returning. Nothing was said at the trials about the men returning after changing their clothes nor the fact that they dressed again in their own clothes. Indeed this would hardly accord with the prosecution case that Joseph had found two strange coats, produced as evidence, and that his own was missing. A further mystery raised by the letter is that Vickerman states that two of the men involved are 'Joseph Mellor's brother who lives at Huddersfield...and a young man who lives [with the] said Wood, whose wife is the young man's mother.' The latter reference is obviously to George Mellor, but what of Joseph's brother? He did have a brother, John, a year younger than George, who may also have been involved in Luddism. It also seems strange that if Vickerman and his nephew had so much information they were not brought as witnesses - in fact, young Vickerman seems to have been the only one of Mellor's apprentices not to be called. [54]

The mystery surrounding the Horsfall shooting is further compounded by doubt cast on whether the manufacturer was in fact the planned target. John Nowell of Farnley Wood, a close friend of the Taylor brothers of Marsden foundry, remembered 1812 well, and was adamant that it was not Horsfall but Enoch Taylor who was the intended victim. Taylor and Horsfall usually rode home together from Huddersfield market but, on that fateful Tuesday of 28 April, Taylor was delayed in Huddersfield by some of his friends, including Nowell and Foster of Wakefield. If true, this piece of information turns the entire prosecution case on its head. This was alluded to by Hobkirk, author of the first history of Huddersfield, enquiring of Nowell in 1867 the basis of his story. 'Could you give me your reasons for saying so as Sowden and Walker in their evidence distinctly state that Mellor said "he was going to shoot Horsfall" and asked them to go with him to shoot Horsfall ?' Unfortunately Nowell's reply has not survived, but Hobkirk thought the anecdote valid enough to record in his *History*. [55]

Perhaps the saddest and most poignant comment on all the confusion and injustice committed in the name of the repression of Luddism appears in the Huddersfield Parish Records. Here, at the bottom of the page recording the burial of John Ogden of Cowcliffe on 18 January 1813, a note has been added describing him and James Haigh of Dalton, buried the following day, as 'Luddites or framebreakers, hanged at York with several others for an attack upon Rawfolds Mill'. This is written in the same hand as other interpolations recording against the burial of John Booth, on 16 April 1812, 'mortally wounded in attempting with a large company of Luddites to destroy Rawfolds Mill' and alongside that of Horsfall on 2 May, 'shot by Luddites on Crosland Moor three of whom were hanged for murder'. But a different hand has added a further note in the margin next to the name of John Ogden :

> *' This man was hung as a Luddite, innocent, but knowing his brother was guilty, but would not inform.'* [56]

To how many more young men, who lost life or liberty as a consequence of the government's desire to crush an incipient revolution, might such a tragic epitaph apply. What chance did any man have, once caught in the terrible machinery of a state which did not hesitate to use any methods of terrorism against its own people, or attempt to distinguish innocent from guilty in its desire to make examples and instill fear? But legal retribution failed to quell the revolutionary spirit of the area, as events over the following eight years were to show.

DEATH OR LIBERTY
The Road To Folly Hall 1813-1817

George Mellor showed the Luddites' concern about wider political issues by forwarding his own and fellow prisoners' names to Tom Ellis, for addition to a parliamentary reform petition. Of course, this can not be used as retrospective evidence that the Luddites had been fighting for reform. But it does show that they were in tune with current political events - and if this was the case while they were in gaol in early 1813, with more pressing worries on their minds, then why not over the previous twelve months, while they were engaged in an armed struggle? The friendship between Ellis, who was helping organise defence witnesses, and Mellor, would indicate that not all the reformers kept Luddism at arms length. Radcliffe suspected that Ellis was in fact deeply implicated in Luddism and had fired the warning shot to intimidate Joseph Mellor.

Major John Cartwright, the veteran campaigner who was primarily responsible for the revival of the reform movement, saw overt workers' political societies as a means of 'turning the discontents into a legal channel favourable to Parliamentary Reform.' Cartwright entered into 'communication with persons connected with the disturbed districts,' including the Huddersfield linen draper, Samuel Clay, and, on 21 January (soon after the York executions), visited the town. A small group of men, some of 'humble station' visited him 'to pay their respects to the good old Gentleman...and to talk about Parliamentary Reform.' Although it was a private meeting the military commander insisted on attending and demanded a copy of the petition under discussion. Those present were taken before Radcliffe and fined for tippling. Such harrassment by the authorities dogged the growth of the reform movement. Commenting on this incident, Lascelles voiced the opinion of many of the ruling class that 'Those who are conversant with the expression "Parliamentary Reform" mean a revolution, indeed, Mr Cartwright's draft of the Petition is pretty explicit upon this subject both in terms and spirit.' It is not suprising that such attitudes meant that repression was often the response to even legal attempts at reform. [1]

Attempts to root out any disloyal sentiments continued. James Chapman, a Bradley Mill dyer, was indicted for sedition in April 1813. Whilst drunk in a pub at Royds Hall he allegedly declared, in praise of Cartwright and reform, 'Damn the King, he is superannuated and has been so for the last twenty and six years. We are governed by nothing but a set of damned whores, rogues and thieves.' He was acquitted after the defence successfully pleaded the Englishman's 'undoubted right' to talk politics in a pub, and evidence revealed that the indiscreet conversation had been encouraged by Whitehead, the Huddersfield constable, acting outside his jurisdiction.[2]

The first local indication of mass agitation following the Ludd outbreak was a petition from the town against the Corn Laws in May 1814, containing 12,322 signatures. From the end of the war the economic situation continued to deteriorate, with an increasing number of bankruptcies, including Ingham's bank in 1816. The introduction of gig mills and shear frames accelerated adding to the plight of the croppers. Luddism was not extinct, only dormant. After an incident of tenter breaking at Longroyd Bridge in May 1813, when Richard Brook was arrested for 'breaking and stealing the iron pins of a tenter belonging to John Drake,' Radcliffe had a two year respite. Then in March 1815, he received a letter from an anonymous informer, warning, 'Ludding is going to start here again...' and that 'old Bellsybub' Radcliffe, Atkinson, Cartwright, Vickerman, Hirst 'and every other Devil that allows machinery' would be shot. An Irishcropper, Jimmy 'Gabbler' Rourke, was said to call himself General Ludd and serve as a delegate to Leeds and elsewhere, while Sam Brook, of Deighton, was also one of the 'principal men of the Ludders'. This could be dismissed as a hoax, or a personal feud against Rourke, but for the attack which happened almost a year later, when frames, shears and windows were smashed at John Robert's cropping shop at Quarmby. A troop of Dragoons was stationed in the town and J.Littlewood, the former adjutant of the Militia, proposed himself as Deputy Barrack Master 'by reason of the Shear-breakers having commenced their destructive Warfare against the obnoxious machinery as they chuse to call it.' The alarm lasted only a few months. If Rourke was really involved it would provide an interesting direct link with Ireland. Along with James Connolly, a horse dealer, and Martin Webb, a master clothdresser and merchant, Rourke was one of the first Irishmen to settle in the town. Webb later entered into partnership with William Swaine, who was reputed to have taken part in the attack on Rawfolds. Another Luddite, whose name indicates he was Irish, and who was thought to have escaped in 1812 by fleeing to Ireland, was Lawrence Gaffney. It is possible that these men, Patrick Doring, and other immigrants brought with them stories of the United Irishmen, or of rural, secret, oath-bound societies such as the Defenders, even if they had not themselves been directly involved in the organisations, adding a further dimension to Huddersfield's subversive, republican culture.[3]

On 23 October 1816 the Huddersfield Union for Parliamentary Reform held what was probably its inaugural meeting. The agreed resolutions were published in the form of a handbill, circulated as widely as Leeds. Radcliffe was informed in December that there were 'seditious meetings frequently held in Huddersfield under the garb of Parliamentary Reform,' and that a public meeting was to be held in the Market Place on the 11th. A bad harvest had deepened the winter privations, contributing to the popularity of the reform movement. In early December a meeting 'numerously attended by both rich and poor', was held at Holmfirth, under the chairmanship of the Rev. Keeling, to discuss measures to alleviate the distress. Reports were given on the condition of the neighbourhood, including a list of the number of looms idle in Wooldale, compiled by Jonathan Wadsworth, a middle class Reformer. When Keeling proposed charitable relief for the destitute, objections were raised that 'it would do well for the present, but... nothing would be so efficacious as parliamentary reform...' He therefore vacated the chair in favour of John Bates, while the meeting proceeded to discuss the political question. John Bates, a manufacturer of Whinney Bank, Scholes, had chaired a peace meeting at Holmfirth in 1808, and may have been the man of that name interrogated about Luddism. Keeling, who had played a part in the suppression of Luddism by informing Constable Blythe about John Schofield's attempt to recruit John Hinchliffe, remained wary of any sentiments smacking of sedition.[4]

It was on the way home from this meeting that Richard Lee, a clothier, said he was first approached by the cropper, Ben Whiteley, and others, about holding meetings in his house. Whiteley was unable to hold them at his own home since 'because he had been taken up as a Luddite folks did not go.' Lee agreed. It was to be a fateful decision for both him and Whiteley. The first meeting at Lee's was called by public advertisement on Friday 26 December, when a *Union Club* was established on the lines set out in a copy of the articles of the Huddersfield Union brought along by Whiteley. Twelve men were on the committee, including Lee, while John Hanson, Lee's brother in law, acted as secretary and George Exley was chosen treasurer, to collect a penny a month subscription from the thirty or so members, who also loaned money for the initial running costs of the club. Their first venture was support for a large public meeting at Holmfirth on 22 January.

The previous week, after the refusal of the Constable to grant a requisition to 127 ratepayers for a meeting in the town, the Huddersfield Union convened a gathering in a steep field on the outskirts. An estimated 7,000 were present including small farmers, a great number of clothiers and other master manufacturers, under the chairman Abraham Hanson, of Elland. Sam Clay read, at length, nineteen resolutions embracing all the main arguments for reform including a call for the unity of 'all classes of Society' to remedy a level of distress 'without precedent'. The blame was placed not on the post-war slump but on the conflict which had preceded it:

> **'the present lamentable situation of affairs is not occasioned**
> **by "a sudden transition from War to Peace" as has been falsely stated, but is**
> **the result of a long, protracted and ruinous War to subjugate the Liberties**
> **both of this and other Nations.'**

War had accelerated the growth of a large standing army, 'calculated to increase the power of the Crown and abridge the Liberty of the Subject.' and augumented the burden of debt incurred by the whole parasitic establishment of 'boroughmongers,' placemen, pensioners, sinecurists and civil list beneficiaries who comprised the state. One clause summarised the underlying political philosophy of the reformers.

> **'That in searching for the immediate cause of the national misery we trace its source to the measures of government...if the general prosperity and happiness of a nation be indicative of a good government, poverty and wretchedness must indicate a bad one.'**

Raising the cry of the American Revolution, 'taxation without representation' was condemned as a violation of the constitution and, whilst asserting that they wished 'to avoid Excesses and Disturbances,' it was stressed 'that nothing short of radical reform will be effectual.' A menacing tone crept into the preamble to the petition, warning of the 'Danger of Anarchy and the Horrors of Civil War' as the 'inevitable tendency' of the frustration of constitutional methods. The meeting decided to adjourn until after Parliament had convened and then, if no positive answer to the petition was forthcoming, to adjourn from Monday to Monday until it was. Alarmed, the *Mercury* noted that this proposal, adopted at several meetings, originated at Spa Fields, London. Since a demonstration there on 2 December had erupted into a riot, it was a recommendation 'which suggests more matter for caution than imitation.' [5]

Thanks were voted to the Hampden Club in London and to the pantheon of leaders - Burdett, Cartwright, Cochrane, Cobbett and Hunt - apparently oblivious to the serious differences about aims and methods which existed among leaders at national level. There was no unanimity about what the movement should do if petitioning failed. Radical reformers like Clay had stated a clear objective of universal suffrage, but drew the line at how far they were prepared to go to achieve it. At least two other speakers inclined towards those becoming known as the 'Ultra-radicals', who considered illegal clandestine methods acceptable if there was no other way. Tom Vevers, a Dalton woolstapler, already had a reputation as a Jacobin, while John Johnston, a tailor from Manchester, was a reform missionary delegated by a meeting at Middleton. The transformation from Political Union to underground revolutionary movement at Middleton is vividly described in Samuel Bamford's autobiography, and it is clear that, via Johnston, the Huddersfield area had direct links with the Lancashire Radicals. Johnston's speech was described as most violent by the *Leeds Intelligencer*, which added sinister innuendo by asserting that he had a 'Gallic accent' and was 'generally thought to be of foreign descent' ![6]

After the Huddersfield meeting, Ben Whiteley asked Johnston to speak the following week at Holmfirth,and a lad with a horse was sent to meet him at Holthead. On 22 January a 'vast multitude' supported resolutions similar to those passed at Huddersfield, including the additional point that 'people can scarcely obtain the necessaries of life...' and a condemnation of those who denied the right to petition 'by Intimidation, Loss of Employment, or any Species of Persecution', as 'Enemies to their Constitution, traitors to their Country...' Johnston stayed the night at Whiteley's and was given a guinea expenses out of the Union Club funds.[7]

Under the influence of the Huddersfield Reform Union, organisation was extended to some other outlying districts. A delegate from the town attended an inaugural meeting of a Thornhill Lees Union on 27 January, which adopted a regulation prohibiting 'immoral, inflammatory and unconstitutional language.' Ironically the meeting was held at the Sportman's Arms, which was to be the venue in June for a meeting of West Riding delegates, among them a Thornhill clothier, planning the Radical uprising. [8]

Meanwhile, locally, as nationally, the clouds of reaction were gathering. A Loyal and Social League was formed in Huddersfield by merchants, manufacturers and other respectable residents which issued a declaration signed by the magistrates and vicar condemning 'the wild and dangerous schemes of Universal Suffrage and Annual Parliaments as tending to produce Scenes of Animosity, Riot, Anarchy and Ruin...' Huddersfield Political Union responded defensively at its next meeting on 10 February, by disclaiming any involvement in illegal meetings - but the alarm of local Loyalists was shared by government. A 'Committee of Secrecy,' inquiring into the growth of political unrest, identified the Reform Unions with the Ultra Radical Spencean Clubs which intended 'not only the overthrow of all political institutions of the Kingdom, but also...a subversion of the rights and principles of property...' A few days after this sensationalist report, on 4 March, the Habeas Corpus Act was suspended, permitting internment without trial. The right of public assembly was also restricted by the Seditious Meetings Act. It was not democracy, but its denial, which was to lead to scenes of animosity and riot. [9]

Johnston was in the forefront of resistance to the repressive legislation, playing a leading role in organising an intended march from Manchester to London on 10 March by those who became known as the 'blanketeers,' from the blankets they carried for the journey. Fearing it was an attempt at insurrection, although the blanketeers carried only walking sticks, the authorities carried out hundreds of arrests, removing Johnston and other Manchester leaders from the political scene. One of his close comrades, who retained his liberty and played a major role in subsequent events, was Joseph Mitchell of Liverpool. The Manchester Radicals went underground, but had been infiltrated by informers. A meeting at Ardwick on 28 March to plan an insurrection was raided and the delegates arrested. One of them, John Lancashire, a Middleton weaver, kept a pike in his house which Sam Bamford hastened to destroy as highly incriminating evidence. On his release from six months of solitary confinement in Chelmsford gaol, Lancashire came to live at Almondbury Bank where, three years later, his reputation almost got him into trouble again. [10]

The Manchester revolutionaries certainly thought they had trans-Pennine support. At a meeting at Chadderton on 23 March a delegate said he had been to Huddersfield and Leeds and 'he was confident the people were all ready to begin at any hour as they had been getting up a deal of arms that had been hid since the time of the Luddites.' It is feasible that links had been maintained even after Johnson was arrested since, as in Lancashire, the Ultra-radicals had gone underground. Holmfirth Political Union, which now had between one and two hundred members, was 'broken up' voluntarily and its books burnt. This proved a wise precaution in the light of a search made on the house of a weaver John Whitehead, of Yew Green, Lockwood, by the Huddersfield constable, when papers were seized. The revelations about the 'Ardwick conspiracy' threw the authorities into alarm, and the newly formed Huddersfield Yeomanry gallantly offered to protect the town while the regular troops were moved into the Manchester area. The *Mercury* was sceptical about the seriousness of the threat, but warned that if the government continued to ignore 'the voice of the people...sham plots may and probably will, soon be changed into real ones.' [11]

Whether or not the Huddersfield radicals were involved in the Lancashire preparations in March, it is indisputable that they were already planning an insurrection before the arrival of the government spy and agent provocateur, William Oliver, at the end of April. As in Lancashire, it was more militant members of the outlawed reform societies who took the lead. George Dawson, a listing maker of Folly Hall, who emerged as one of the leading revolutionaries, first approached Michael Waller, later a Roberttown delegate, with a request to sign the petition at the first Huddersfield mass reform meeting. Tom Riley, who as we have seen, narrowly escaped Radcliffe's clutches for his support for Luddism, later recollected that the question of a rising had first been mentioned at a meeting with the innocuous object of discussing the payment of a bill for advertising expenses in the *Mercury*. Lee and Whiteley, instrumental in forming the Reform Club in Holmfirth, were foremost in planning the insurrection in that district. Local radicals were quite capable of deciding for themselves that an uprising was the only course left open. They did not need a government agent to sow the seed in their minds, or to concoct a totally spurious conspiracy to ensnare them. Oliver was, however, guilty of encouraging their hopes with completely false reports of the support expected from other areas, particularly the capital. [12]

John Buckley, a shoemaker of Longroyd Bridge, first heard of the intended rising in early April when, on a visit to Dawson's house, he was told by him 'petitioning was of no use and therefore there is a plan formed to overthrow the present system of government.' George Taylor, later the Honley delegate, was also there and already party to the plan. Prompted by Mrs Dawson, he confirmed 'the business was going forward well and would put the country to rights.' Someone called Liddell had donated one pound, and two pounds had been given by people at Lockwood to buy gunpowder to make ball cartridges. Dawson had brewed ale and bought some rum, to put the men in the right 'spirits'. Buckley, like all those subsequently interrogated, was reticent about his own role. Riley claimed that he himself had only been to two meetings, but had refused to join because of his doubts about the success of a venture known to too many people. He was in contact with a delegate however, who had been to 'central meetings' at the Yew Tree, Roberttown and in Honley Wood. Although he claimed he only told one person at Honley and two at Longwood about the plan, other witnesses attributed a more active role to him. William Schofield, of Honley, said that, in the course of a conversation about 'trade and such like and the badness of the times and the upper country [Manchester] disturbances...' Riley had revealed that there was to be a general rising, and a few days before the event he commented to Schofield 'I expect you will be there'. Buckley claimed he had frequently been approached by Riley 'to join or bring about the Revolution as he termed it' and was offered the use of an old halberd, reputedly 'used in Ludding time.' Riley had also given him lead and a bullet mould to prepare ball. If Riley had already made clear his opposition to the plan, this does not explain why, on his own admission, he was asked to be a delegate to a meeting with men from the Hampden Club, nor why the man who went in his place should have confided in him what went on.

The men from the 'Hampden Club' were, in fact, Joseph Mitchell and William Oliver, who certainly did not represent the Hampden Club, but did have genuine links with London Radicals. It is not clear how far they represented any actual organisation in the capital, since the most revolutionary body likely to be involved, the Spencean Society, had been paralysed by the arrest of its leader, Arthur Thistlewood, and his comrades. Via Birmingham and Derby, Mitchell and Oliver arrived in Sheffield on 26 April and moved on to Wakefield the following day, where they met delegates at Ben Scholes' pub, the *Joiner's Arms*. They found district committees in existence at these places, which occasionally sent delegates to central meetings. Huddersfield maintained links built up by the Radicals from the days of open campaigning for the Reform Unions, including Leeds, Sheffield, the Spen Valley, Ossett, Wakefield and possibly Barnsley. Halifax is notable by its absence at this time and Riley offered a cryptic explanation 'Halifax would put no confidence in Huddersfield on account of Ludding times. Halifax corresponded with Sheffield, when a delegate attended from Huddersfield there was none from Halifax.' Whether this is a reference to the confusion over the attack on Rawfolds - although on this occasion it was the Huddersfield men who were let down by the late appearance of the Halifax contingent - or some other antagonism, it is interesting that some Radicals felt that they were continuing the Luddite struggle.

Although organisation existed within the West Riding, and probably with adjacent manufacturing districts, there is no evidence of direct links with London other than through Mitchell, which accords with Bamford's account of his role and Oliver's appraisal of him as the 'principal agent of communication.' How well Mitchell was known in the Huddersfield area before this time is not known. He certainly had a contact in the district since, on 4 May, returning from Liverpool for a delegate meeting at Wakefield, he got off the coach near Huddersfield to visit someone, only to be arrested by Special Constables at Golcar. Consequently, from now on, liason between the different manufacturing districts was mainly carried out by 'the London delegate,' Mr Oliver. [13]

The major meeting, for which Mitchell was returning, went ahead in his absence at Wakefield the next day. Tom Bacon, a veteran Republican and Luddite suspect, from Pentrich in Derbyshire, was present, fresh from a meeting with Bamford at Middleton. Sheffield was represented by William Wolstenholme and Horbury by John Smaller - both had been members of United English committees in 1802, and Smaller was suspected of being a 'notorious stealer of arms' in 1812. There were delegates from Birmingham, Leeds and Barnsley. George Dawson,and someone called Sykes, attended from Huddersfield. Vastly inflated reports of the radicals' strength in the respective districts was given - Dawson said they could raise 8,000 men in the Huddersfield area. The next day Oliver went to Huddersfield to see Mitchell who, after 26 hours in the Towser, - 'the most damp and nauseous dungeon imaginable, having no fire in it, the floor of which was nearly covered with human excrement' - was moved to a room and allowed visitors. Mitchell asked Oliver to call on friends, including Dawson, who passed on to him a letter from the prisoner to his wife in Liverpool. This is the first evidence of Oliver directly visiting revolutionaries in the town. According to the *Mercury*'s expose of his role he also met George Taylor, but after twice trying unsuccesfully to arrange meetings with other local Radicals he told Ben Scholes that he was 'dissatisified with the apathy of the country.' He had more hopes in the people of Ossett, which he toured with Smaller on 10 May, as they appeared 'more desperate than any others.' [14]

On Sunday 11 May a central meeting was held near Roberttown which John Buckley of Longroyd Bridge attended, along with an unnamed delegate from Almondbury. Three days later at a Sheffield meeting, whether because of apprehension about the state of preparedness among local leaders, or due to a wrecking tactic by Oliver, it was suddenly decided to postpone the rising from Whit Monday, 26 May, until 9 June, ostensibly to avoid a night of the full moon. Wolstenholme requested Tom Bradley, who was in fact another informer, to convey the news to delegates at a meeting at Thurlestone on Sunday the 18th. Despite the fact that Holmfirth delegates had already complained to Wolstenholme about the fatigue and expense of all the meetings, only Holmfirth and Huddersfield men arrived at the *Waggon & Horses* - Ben Whiteley, Joseph Beaumont of Scholes and a Lockwood man, all of them croppers. Recognising

Bradley by a blue ribbon in his button hole, they initiated conversation. Whiteley expressed concern that the Barnsley lads 'were rather too forward', and asked that Wolstenholme give an answer to a man in Sheffield who had offered to make sixty pikes in return for payment in cloth. A Sheffield proposal to seize Wentworth House and an arms depot in Doncaster was agreed, with Whiteley promising to send a Huddersfield detachment to help. [15]

Although this plan may have emanated from Oliver it was similar to the tactics proposed elsewhere. In Huddersfield, a plan to raid Milnsbridge House and take the 30 stand of arms stored there was attributed to Tom Vevers by John Buckley, who said that Vevers had asked him, as an ex-soldier, to lead the attack. At Hightown, Ben Hepponstall, a cropper and old friend of Riley, was to capture Cartwright and the Rev. Roberson - both leading adversaries of the Luddites-while, according to Bradley, Smaller planned to attack Bretton Hall where 100 stand of arms were kept and to seize the town halls and House of Correction. Thus well armed and with the magistrates and other main opponents captured, the revolutionaries expected to surround and disarm the military garrisons with little resistance. Their confident attitude was summed up by Whiteley, who asserted that 'the rising would be general of all the nation and once they were agate there would be plenty of force.' Although Oliver may have misled the Radicals over the level of support to be expected from London, he cannot be blamed for fostering delusions about local strength. Nor can the details of preparations be traced to him. None of the schemes which came to light would have stretched the imagination of local revolutionaries - Tom Riley, for example, had been dreaming up plans for at least five years. Even if Oliver had never appeared on the scene the rising would have gone ahead, since the Radicals had wildly optimistic views of the revolutionary mood of the people. The fact that some persisted with the scheme, even after it became evident things had gone terribly wrong, testifies to this misjudgement. [16]

After the postponement of the rising there were at least two more meetings in Sheffield. The last of these, on 30 May, was raided by magistrates acting on information from Bradley. Although only 4 out of the 30 or so delegates were apprehended, it must have been apparent that the arrest of Wolstenholme would seriously affect Sheffield's contribution to the rising. Michael Waller, a collier and publican of Roberttown, visited Dawson on Tuesday 3 June and found him and his wife selling listing near the Cloth Hall. The men adjourned to the Kings Head, and then to a pub in the Shambles, to discuss the situation. Dawson asked Waller to attend an afternoon meeting at the *Sportman's Arms*, Thornhill Lees, to finalise arrangements on the afternoon of 6 June. Again, due to intelligence from Bradley, this was turned into a trap by the authorities. Ten delegates were arrested, including Whiteley, Waller, Smaller, Joshua Midgeley an Almondbury clothier, William Walker a Thornhill Lees clothier and James Mann a Leeds cropper and prominent radical, along with others from Manningham, Wakefield and Hightown. They were escorted into Wakefield by a troop of Yeoman Cavalry, who were stoned, while an 'immense assemblage' gathered around the Court House, indicative of the strong popular sympathy which the revolutionaries hoped to tap.[17]

Oliver was also at the *Sportman's Arms,* but managed to escape with the connivance of General Byng, the northern military commander, now aware of the role of the Home Secretary's spy. A few hours later, John Dickinson, a Dewsbury linen draper and radical, who had refused to become involved in the rising, saw him in Wakefield speaking to Byng's coachman. Via Leeds, Oliver travelled to Nottingham and on to London. Amazingly, although the Thornhill arrests, on top of those at Sheffield, had practically smashed the revolutionary organisation in the West Riding, some of the Holmfirth and Huddersfield radicals resolved to carry on partly in desperation.

A weekend of frenetic activity ensued. The evening of the arrests, Friday 6 June, Dawson was supping ale when he saw a party of soldiers approaching. Alarmed, he went into hiding somewhere near Moldgreen. The next day Riley anxiously sought a copy of the *Mercury* to find out what was happening. It carried the story of the arrests under the heading *'Rumours of Threatened Insurrection,'* but no mention of Dickinson's revelations about Oliver. Whether it would have made any difference had it done so is impossible to say, but it was a source of Radical resentment against the editor, Edward Baines, for years to come. Riley's response would indicate that some revolutionaries were set on their course, telling Buckley that 'all was up for the plan was completely broken into...it must either be done now or we shall all be hanged.' Dawson sent a message, asking Buckley to go to Manchester, and Riley agreed that they had to ensure that the people there, 'must be ready to strike at the time appointed.' Dawson's wife also urged him to go, saying 'something must be done or all these poor men will be hanged.' Why Buckley was asked to do this, if he was as little involved as he later claimed, is not clear. He had already shown a lack of enthusiasm by not making the bullets he had been asked to prepare. Only the day before Riley had angrily demanded the mould back, saying 'Give me the stuff and I will take it to where it will be done.' Buckley set off for Manchester and on the way overtook Ben Heponstall, engaged on a similar mission. Evidently the revolutionaries were less well informed than General Byng, who reported to the Home Office on 4 June that Manchester had abandoned its plans following the Sheffield arrests. George Taylor, of Honley, also travelled on horseback over Holme Moss to relay news of the Thornhill arrests and seek support in Stockport.

Meanwhile, Richard Lee at Holmfirth, found out at seven o'clock on Saturday morning that Whiteley had not returned home, but he did not hear of the arrests until midday. A stranger from Huddersfield, an ex-soldier or sailor, 'a queer fellow' according to Haigh, apparently sent by Dawson, brought the news and asked Lee if he could get the information to Sheffield. Lee took him to Joseph Beaumont at Scholes who wrote a note for Thomas Beaumont (then staying at a pub near Sheffield bullring), and escorted the stranger to Jackson Bridge to put him on the Sheffield road. About half past three in the afternoon a worker from Wakefield House of Correction arrived in Holmfirth with a letter from Whiteley for his wife. (This may be the messenger on horseback referred to by Haigh). She was working at John Bates' at Whinney Bank, and the man waited in Whiteley's house, while the children went to fetch her. One of Lee's children was with them and told Richard, who read the already opened letter. Whilst someone was writing a reply, Lee, anticipating his own arrest, went to John Hirst's of Liphill Bank to borrow a gun, telling Hirst's wife he needed it for self-defence, but she refused to lend it.

The next morning Lee went to see Mrs Whiteley, who set of for Joseph Mellor's at Burnlee to try to raise bail for Ben. When he returned, the clothier, Richard Haigh, called with two Honley men, one a cropper, who inquired, 'who they were to apply to about the business', now Whiteley was arrested. They wanted to know whether Holmfirth would join them or not, and went to a pub at Upper Bridge to await a reply, and the return of George Taylor from 'the upper country'. About four o'clock, Lee called together John Langley, of Deanhouse, and some other former Club members, asserting that petitioning was useless and force had to be used - 'all the force was to be mustered that possibly could that night, for delays were dangerous.' He said two men were waiting for an answer. 'We must go lads for it will do nothing dodging on it, the business must be done tonight.' They were to fight for liberty and march on Huddersfield - 'there is nothing at all to stop us.' He thought there was a great deal of dependable support in Holmfirth and neighbourhood. Joseph Beaumont claimed that a number of ball cartridges had been made every night for some weeks, and that Hepworth, Scholes and New Mill could probably raise more force than Holmfirth. He said that the plan was to place a guard at Honley, Lockwood and Engine Bridges. Jonathan Bailey, of Pog Ing, suggested that Banks at Honley would be the best place to meet.

Lee later claimed that he had shown less enthusiasm. When, at the time 'Chapel loosed', the Honley men returned for a reply, they explained the departure from the plan to rise on the following night, the 9th - the 'business was to be done that night as there was a watch Monday night.' Lee complained that they had no arms to go with. One replied 'they had plenty and if they had not they would begin a Ludding' and seize guns from those who would not accompany them - 'they would take all the guns they could find at Honley as they went and then they would come to Huddersfield and seize the soldiers' arms...it would not be above ten minutes work.' Lee was still unconvinced. Between eight and nine that evening he went to George Exley's to borrow a pistol. Although he later said it was only for his own defence, at the time he gave a different impression to John

Langley, to whom he showed the pistol and said grimly 'It was to be death or liberty that night.' In the event he did not turn up at the rendezvous, claiming afterwards that his wife was ill and his house under surveillance. Richard Haigh and Exley, also fearing arrest, slept that night at Abraham Bailey's house at Cliffe. Isaac Johnson and Joshua Thewles, labourers, tried unsuccesfully to borrow arms. Johnson told Langley that he would show 'he could prime and load as sharp as some of them.' Thewles said he would go to join the rising, although he knew nothing of military discipline. Late that evening Samuel Wimpenny, a weaver, was heading home with Jonathan Fallas to the latter's father's house where they both lodged. Isaac Johnson, who lodged with Wimpenny's brother, called from the window for them to go and get ready and he would meet them at the bottom of the lane. But when Samuel got home and had his supper, he began to undress for bed. Johnson called to the house and warned 'It would be either life or death if people did not go and they would be safer there than at home.' With persuasion from Fallas, Wimpenny consented to go at least as far as Banks. John Donkersley was also called on, and accompanied Johnson, Thewlis and the others to Banks. About 30 to 40 men gathered with only seven or eight guns and pistols between them. Wimpenny recognised only a few other Holmfirth men, including Joseph Beaumont and someone called Cockin. Donkersley said he was given a gun by George Taylor.

George Taylor had as good an excuse as any for failing to turn out that evening after a gruelling ride over the Pennines and back. Warned at Holme of the danger of arrest, he had returned via Scholes and had his horse sent back by another route. Whether he met the Honley men in the pub, and was with them when they returned to Lee's is not clear, since he was apparently back at Hall Ing chapel by late afternoon or early evening when he told John Oldham, a labourer of Marsh Platt, of the rendezvous that night. Taylor was described by one witness as 'little Taylor', but whether this referred to his stature or meant junior is not evident. Oldham referred to him as 'the huntsman's son', and a George Taylor, huntsman, Honley, appears in the Parish registers for 1794, when a son, Ben, was baptised. The Taylors therefore had some standing in the community and although George junior's occupation is not mentioned, he was rumoured to have been involved with Luddism, including the attack on Rawfolds. His conduct of the rising seems to indicate some Luddite experience.

John Oldham and George Kay, a mason, unconvincingly claimed that they were on their way home when they were met by men with guns and compelled to 'fall in'. Joseph Sykes was alerted by a rap on his door at Berry Croft, but took a long time getting ready, complaining he couldn't find his breeches, and when Butterworth called on Joshua Hirst to get ready, his wife, Mary, rushed off to inform the Honley constable George Thurgoland. On her way back she bumped into some of the insurgents and had the audacity to order them to disperse, announcing she was a Special Constable. One swore, 'Damn her, drop her!' but she was not harmed. Joshua Kemp, an 18 year old clothier, also said he was at Thirstin on his way home near eleven, when Taylor and Uriah Butterworth asked him to join, the latter saying 'if he would go to Honley bridge he would see a great many people as something was going to be done at Huddersfield.' Kemp found only ten men at Honley Bridge and another 20 to 30, whom he presumed were Holmfirth men, at Far End, Banks. Some wanted to go home, others said they would not go to Huddersfield without firearms, and he recollected that it was Taylor who suggested that they first march into Honley to collect guns. Two sentinels were placed on the bridge, while the main body marched into Honley with the gunmen in the front.

John Donkersley said he was placed on look out at Shambles as the raids on houses began, first at William and Godfrey Sanderson's. Hearing the demand 'a brace of pistols or your life,' the guns were handed over. William Leigh of Church Street had his kitchen window smashed, but refused to leave the security of his bedroom, and Ben Varley heard banging at the door and the threat, which Kemp testified to as being made by a man carrying a scythe, of 'Bring Enoch forward.' That a sledge hammer should be referred to by its Luddite nickname is another confirmation of the enduring tradition. Varley cautiously put his gun out butt first, without opening the door wide. Joseph Armitage surrendered three guns, one of which was found at Far End on the following Tuesday. Sarah Jessop's husband was away and, although her son and son in law were in the house, she was apprehensive about admitting the men who threatened to break in, saying, 'I am a married woman I hope you will behave yourselves.' Someone assured her 'We will.' A tall, dark man lit a candle, and pulled his hat low over his eyes as they searched the house, but could not find the guns she had hastily hidden. Courteously, on leaving, they wished the occupants good night. The revolutionaries had the most trouble at the house of Clement Dyson, the man who had been raided twice in 1812, when living at Dungeon. As on a former occasion it was Hannah, his wife, who confronted the attackers, Clement being away on business. Someone knocked on the door with the demand 'Your firelock, immediately,' but she claimed there wasn't a gun in the house. After threats to smash in the door, she went to the garret to fetch the pistol her husband had got for defence against the Luddites. Entry had been forced by the time she came downstairs with the weapon. 'You are a damned set of Ludding rogues,' she said as she handed it over, ' you will never be quiet until you are hung in a string.' Someone impolitely suggested they 'blow a ball through her,' but she was left fuming, as they formed up in order and marched off.

The main body collected the guards from Honley Bridge and marched off in ranks towards Huddersfield. It was at some point that George Taylor reputedly urged them on with his oft quoted speech, 'Now Lads, all England is in arms - our liberties are secure - The rich will be poor and the poor will be rich!' About half an hour's brisk march took them via Northgate to Taylor Hill.[18]

Men from Berry Brow, Lockwood and the vicinity had meanwhile gathered near Folly Hall, knocking up supporters on the way. Some, like Nathan Taylor, a shoemaker of Well Green, claimed later that it was under duress they left their homes that night. Taylor said he was awakened about one o'clock by men threatening to break the door open and told to get dressed and come with them. They refused at first to say where to, but, after a plea from Taylor's wife, replied Huddersfield. He went with them as far as Knowle Hill where, with another man, he 'escaped'. He only saw three or four persons with a couple of scythes and a gun. Another shoemaker, George Armitage, said that he had been to Lockwood courting and, with Charles Earnshaw, was returning to Huddersfield about 12 o'clock, when at Engine Bridge by two men levelling guns at him. He was told to come into the field as they were seeing how many they could muster that night. 'Must we?' asked Earnshaw. 'If you do not come over we will shoot you' one of the men allegedly replied. Since Earnshaw was not called as a prosecution witness there is no corroboration for Armitage's statement. It is highly unlikely that the insurgents would want any unreliable persons with them who had been coerced. It is more likely that some half-hearted supporters were persuaded, against their better judgement, to turn out that night. On being arrested they were the ones most likely to give evidence which absolved themselves from any complicity.

For whatever reason, Armitage was in the field at Folly Hall which, by coincidence, belonged to his father. He later told people, whilst denying he had been present himself, that over three hundred were present. Only eight or nine had guns and pistols according to his evidence, which seems a very low proportion of firearms if there were hundreds there. Ammunition was distributed from handkerchiefs on the wall, and then the men moved from the field onto Engine Bridge, with Joseph Croft in command. Armitage identified the Lockwood croppers John Wilson, aged 19, and George Woffenden, 22, with firearms, and Joseph Jysop, 21, with a scythe. As two horsemen were spotted coming down Chapel Hill, Croft ordered those with guns to kneel on each side of the road on the bridge, facing the town. Captain Armitage, commander of the recently formed Huddersfield Yeomanry, a volunteer body of well-to-do merchants, manufacturers and tradesmen, had been alerted to the suspicious activities at Folly Hall. Summoning six privates and George Whitehead, he rode out towards Engine Bridge to investigate. Privates Alexander and Shires reconnoitred about 50 yards in front. Alexander saw 60 or 70 figures on the bridge and shouted 'There they are!'. What happened next is confused by the pace of events and later controversy.

Whitehead went forward to question the men, but was challenged by Croft who demanded 'Who comes there?' He barely had time to retort 'What are you doing there?' when, possibly after a shot from the Yeomanry, who were nervously riding with pistols drawn, Croft gave the order to fire. The first gun flashed in the pan, but failed to discharge and was followed by a ragged volley. Alexander's grey reeled beneath him with a wound to the head, but recovered, and on Armitage's orders the party galloped back to the town. The insurgents had lost the advantage of suprise, and if any of them had seriously meant to press the attack on the town with their meagre forces, the skirmish at Engine Bridge changed their minds. As the men were dispersing, a gun went off on Taylor Hill, either an insurgent sentinel or the Honley and Holmfirth party announcing their arrival. Someone said, 'Have you nothing to answer it with?' and John Wilson discharged his pistol. The Honley men met some of the retreating insurgents at Taylor Hill and heard that they had been fired on by cavalry. It was probably with a mixed feeling of disappointment and relief that the insurgents returned to their beds.[19]

On the following day, one of the delegates who had been to Manchester (probably Hepponstall), learned of the failure from Riley. 'The damned fools.' he retorted 'they knew it was Monday night.' He was not to know that the outcome would have been no different if the pre-arranged time had been kept, for only one small area was to rise. That night, in the villages around Pentrich in Derbyshire, a scene was enacted similar to the on in the Holme Valley twenty four hours earlier. About 100 framework-knitters, miners, quarrymen and other labourers under Jeremiah Brandreth, marched towards Nottingham gathering forces as they went, but were dispersed the following morning merely by the approach of cavalry. Unfortunately this near farce was marred by a tragedy - the insurgents accidently shot and killed a man at a house where they demanded arms.[20]

Over the following weeks numerous arrests were made in the rebel areas. A detachment of the 13th Dragoons was stationed in Huddersfield to assist the Yeomanry and 130 men of the 33rd Regiment of Foot in rounding up suspects and searching for arms. Fears persisted that the insurgents were planning another attempt, and signal shots and beacons on the hills were reported. About 30 men were held for questioning and then taken under cavalry escort to York Castle.[21]

Although he had not been present at the rising, Tom Riley was accused of, 'procuring, commanding or abetting others to bring about and commit certain riots, unlawful assemblies and felonies' - a charge which was later, on the instructions of the Home Secretary, turned to one of High Treason. Riley expressed great remorse at the failure, allegedly lamenting 'he had for many years kept the law and the government at defiance and now he was betrayed to destruction by a set of his own blockheads.' Whether this is precisely how he expressed his opinion or not, he was certainly so despondent that he tried to hang himself from his bedstead, during his confinement at Huddersfield.[22]

The fears of the revolutionaries were summed up by John Langley, who visited Lee the morning after and told him 'Ludding was very bad, but this was ten times worse, all that were there would be hung.' Lee replied lamely, 'He could not help it - it was done now.' Taylor, Croft, Dawson, Richard Haigh, Uriah Butterworth, Ben Shaw, Jonathan Fallas, and Jonathan Bailey went on the run, and searches for them extended at least as far as Stockport and Manchester. Croft, described by the *Intelligencer* as 'a master shoemaker of Huddersfield in respectable credit and flourishing business,' was rumoured to have reached Hamburg. On the 13 June Richard Lee was arrested. Matthew Bradley, the magistrate's clerk, entered his house with a posse of men and forced him at pistol point to come with them, without even a chance for a wash or to say a few words to his wife. Her illness (she was later 'cut for a cancer' of the breast), added to his anxiety while confined to the Towser, and she was not allowed to see him. He gave a statement, which, although it named some names such as Whiteley, did not incriminate anyone by attributing to them a leading role in the organisation of the rising, or actual involvement in the events of the night. B. H. Allen, the magistrate, and Tom Atkinson, offered him improved conditions if he told all he knew, but he refused to divulge anything else and, after five nights in squalor, he was allowed a better room. On 16 July he was escorted to York in irons to face trial for treason. Ben Whiteley, bailed three weeks after his capture at Thornhill Lees, was re-arrested on 4 July by Blythe the Holmfirth constable, who searched 'every drawer, closet and cranny' of his house. Charged with High Treason, he was committed to Coldbath prison in London and then, following four days of examination before the Home Secretary, was sent to Worcester gaol where he remained for five months. Both Holmfirth men and Riley suffered short but harsh terms of imprisonment without trial. Those who appeared before a jury were more fortunate.[23].

The *Leeds Mercury* had investigated the role of Oliver and condemned the way he, as a government agent, had actually encouraged the revolutionaries by false assurances of support in London. By the time of the York Summer Assizes there was widespread sympathy among even middle class parliamentary reformers for 'Oliver's dupes.' Few of the insurgents turned King's evidence. Samuel Wimpenny, the Holmfirth clothier, claimed he had been pressurised into joining and identified some of his comrades. The main witness against the eight men accused of arms stealing in Honley was Mrs Dyson, who testified that she saw Sykes of Berry Croft among the attackers. George Armitage, the shoemaker, was the main prosecution witness against the Lockwood men, accused of tumultuously assembling at Folly Hall, although a defence witness said that Armitage had confided to him that he was involved, but had not mentioned being coerced, whilst he had told others he hadn't been there at all. Both Armitage and his friend Earnshaw had been in custody for six weeks and, the prosecution's case was severely weakened when they refused to call Earnshaw. He later swore that this was because he had turned down the bribe of a few oranges offered to him to testify that the Yeomanry had definitely not fired first.

Besides the reliability of the prosecution witnesses being challenged a number of respectable character witnesses spoke for the defendants. George Woffenden, a young cropper from Lockwood, was described as a religious man, looking after his widowed mother and 'good, honest, sober and very peacable.' None of the others had had any stain on their character. Fortunately, the political climate had changed since 1812 and hostility to the government outweighed fears of revolution among many of the middle classes. After only a quarter of an hour the jury returned the verdict of not guilty. With a stern warning from the judge about their narrow escape the men promised to watch their future conduct. The esteem in which the liberated men were held was shown on 27 July when they were:

> **'met on their approach to Huddersfield by an immense number of men, women and children who hailed their safe return. The scenes which were exhibited between the men and their families and the boys and their parents at this happy meeting we shall not pretend to describe.'** [24]

Their Derbyshire counterparts were less fortunate - three were hanged and 14 transported for from 14 years to life. The Yorkshire trials also had their tragic sequel. Riley, still in York castle in October, cut his own throat, leaving a widow and ten children. Lee was left to help clean up the suicide cell. He was released at the end of the year, as was Whiteley, just before the Habeas Corpus Suspension Act expired, the government preferring to let the embarrassing episode drop.[25]

The 1817 uprising reveals a high degree of amateurism and self deception amongst the insurgents, but they cannot be dismissed as mere dupes of Oliver. There was a belief widespread among working people that an armed uprising, a march on London and overthrow of the government would establish a democratic political system and economic improvement. Exactly what form this would take may not have been clear to all the participants, although some certainly wanted a Republic. Supporters of the ideas of Thomas Spence desired fundamental economic change, involving the break up and distribution of the great landholdings of the aristocracy, but it is unclear how established the Spenceans were outside London. Mitchell subscribed to their views two years later and may have been propagating them in 1817. Resistance to the further spread of industrialism was undoubtedly one of the unspoken objectives of the rising and it is clear from the numerous references to Luddism that many of the rebels of 1817 considered they were carrying on where those of 1812 left off. Similarly, the experiences of 1817 were taken into account in the preparation of the next rising, after legal outlets of popular protest had again been blocked.

THE GODDESS OF FREEDOM
Revival and Repression of the Mass Movement 1819.

In February 1818 Francis Burdett presided over a meeting at the Hope & Anchor in London, to raise subscriptions for those who had suffered imprisonment without trial. John Johnston and Joseph Mitchell recounted their experiences of arrest and gaol, Mitchell asserting that he had been reduced to beggary but was 'still hearty in the cause as ever,' The fact that he had been visited in gaol by Oliver and, on his release, was to continue political activity without any obvious source of income, was later used to cast suspicion on his role in 1817, and thereby to discredit ultra-radicalism in general. Whiteley and Lee were still writing to the papers in March and April to refute denials that they had been ill-treated. A petition about Riley's case was 'numerously and respectably signed by his friends at Huddersfield' and, as late as February 1819, his nephew remained angry enough to publically answer claims by the *Leeds Independent* that Riley had killed himself because he dared not face trial. It was rather the prospect of indefinite imprisonment without trial that 'sunk his spirits, alienated his reason and destroyed his existence.' [1]

In March the government passed an Indemnity Act to protect its ministers and officials who had acted illegaly whilst enforcing the repressive measures. Repression had worked by disorganising the radicals and increasing dissension within their camp. Seditious meetings, that is any large political gathering, remained illegal until mid 1818. This does not mean that there was general submission to repressive legislation, since there was blatant defiance of the Combination Laws. Although successive years saw some improvement over the trough of the depression in 1816, continuing economic hardship led to an upsurge of worker's militancy, directed not towards political reform, but into the formation of trade unions to win improved wages. In July 1818 there were widespread strikes, or *'turn-outs'*, among cotton spinners and weavers around Manchester and Stockport. In October Barnsley linen weavers struck and paraded the town in military order. The following year colliers from St Helens to Bradford were organising, while Carlisle gingham weavers, complaining that they could only earn 7s a week, held mass meetings on the Solway sands and spread a strike to surrounding villages. In April there was a demonstration of unemployed weavers and croppers in Leeds, and in June a mass meeting on Hunslet Moor. Croppers had been particularly hard hit by the spread of gig-mills and shear frames, and by the return of ex-soldiers saturating the labour market.[2]

In Huddersfield, resentment against machinery continued and, although it may be an example of frustration rather than organised opposition, in October 1818 John Webster was 'violently assaulted' by a cropper, John Bolland,and his brother Ben, 'supposing that he was one of the workmen employed by Messrs Atkinson of Bradley Mills at their Gig Mills.' The prosecution against the Bollands was dropped, due to Atkinson's sympathy for their aged parents, but on the condition that they inserted a 'Pardon Asked' notice in the Leeds papers. Apart from this incident, in contrast to the militancy in surrounding towns, there are no reports of strikes or even disputes in the Huddersfield area. Some local workers must have been in contact with trade unionists since, by the end of 1819, attempts were being made to establish illegal combinations among coal miners at Flockton and Calder Main collieries, and among blanket weavers at Dewsbury. [3]

Although trade unionism could cut both ways, for instance the Radical Dewsbury printer James Willan was reproved by a weaver when he mentioned politics at a union meeting, the workers' economic struggles certainly injected a stronger class content into revived Radicalism. The rights of the 'labourers' or 'labouring part of the people' are regularly asserted in resolutions for reform, and an Address issued in Leeds in July 1819 specifically condemned the 'detestable combination law which at one stroke reduces the whole class of labourers to the degraded condition of most abject slaves.' Mass meetings in 1819, in contrast to those in early 1817, were usually composed mainly of workers and artisans, and regarded with apprehension by the middle classes.[4]

Radicalism's reawakening in the north was signalled by the founding of the Stockport Union Society in October 1818. In January, Henry Hunt visited Manchester with his strategy of mass mobilisation of the people to present a grand remonstrance to the Prince Regent. The role of Huddersfield in the revival of this movement is obscure until delegates from Huddersfield and Holmfirth joined others from all over Lancashire, Yorkshire and the neighbouring districts at Oldham on 7 June to promote the foundation of Union Societies for parliamentary reform. Some embryonic organisation at least probably existed in Huddersfield, and the circulation of the *Manchester Observer* in the town in May, indicates that the revival of radicalism had a ready audience. The resolutions of the Oldham meeting, which, as well as the usual demands for parliamentary reform, referred to low wages and high prices, was adopted by a mass meeting on Hunslet Moor. [5]

By the following month, Union Societies, with the central demand of annual parliaments and universal suffrage, were being organised throughout the West Riding including the Huddersfield area. Joseph Tyas, a weaver, was asked to join one at Rastrick in July, by Tempest Tiffany, a cropper who had been one of those 'untwisted' from the Luddite oath in 1812. Each member paid a penny subscription towards buying literature, including the *Manchester Observer* and the *Black Dwarf*, which were read at weekly meetings at each other's houses. A Deighton cropper, Joshua Hirst, also joined a society organised in a 'class' of 25 members, and paid a penny for publications including the *Cap of Liberty,* as well as those mentioned by Tyas. Within a few months both Hirst and Tyas, through their membership of Union Societies, were to be drawn into preparations for an uprising.[6]

The Union Societies announced their existence in Huddersfield with a notice in the *Mercury* of 24 July, calling a public meeting at one o'clock on Monday 2 August, 'to take into their most serious and calm Consideration the best Means of obtaining Relief from the pressing Burdens which they now labour under and the most effectual Means of securing their Constitutional Rights in the Commons House of Parliament.' The Constable had refused their requisition for a meeting, and therefore it was to be held 'in a FIELD betwixt the River and the Canal near the Dock Yard.' The notice concluded 'we invite our Countrymen to come forward and form a NATIONAL UNION on Constitutional Grounds to support the Pillars of the Constitution of England.' Fourteen workers and artisans were signatories - nine croppers, a clothier, a tailor, a shoemaker, a hatter and a framework knitter. At least two of them, John Gill, cropper, and Joseph Pilling, clothier,(or as he is elsewhere described, fancy weaver) were later to resort to arms.

John Dickinson, the Dewsbury linen draper who had exposed Oliver in 1817, chaired the meeting which convened, not on the advertised spot, but on the steep hillside of Almondbury Bank, where quarrying had carved out a sort of crude arena. Flags were carried emblazoned with *'No Corn Laws'* as well as reform slogans and, amidst cheers, a red cap of liberty, the French revolutionary symbol, was hoisted on the pole of the flag declaring *'Annual Parliaments.'* Tom Mason of Leeds delivered the opening address, quoting Burns to illustrate the simple ideal of contentment denied to the labourer :

> **'His clean hearth stone, his thrifty wife's smile,**
> **The lisping infant prattling on his knee**
> **Did all his weary earking cares beguile,**
> **And made him quite forget his labour and his toil.'**

Instead of this 'The chilling hand of penury has converted his comfortable cottage into a wretched hovel.' His oration concluded in a wave of cheers as, gesturing towards the red cap on the flagpole, he announced 'I see the Goddess of Freedom presented you with that emblem of Liberty!' James Mann, the Leeds cropper arrested at Thornhill Lees in 1817, also won applause with a homespun metaphor for economic exploitation 'Like the industrious bee they had stored the hive and the lazy drones had devoured the honey.' Perhaps the most interesting oratory of the meeting was not recorded. According to the *Mercury*, Bob Harrison of Huddersfield 'read a tedious and violent speech which seemed to give much offence to many of the persons on the hustings, and which, for his sake, as well as to save the patience of our readers, we refrain from publishing.' This Harrison is not mentioned elsewhere, except in a report from the local military commander to general Byng where he is described as a weaver and a 'low and notoriously bad character', whose real name was Broadhurst. The silence of the *Mercury* means we do not know how well his proposals were received by the audience. Mann proposed the formation of Female Reform Unions, and, after the reading of an address by Chris Wood,the meeting closed with three-times-three cheers for Cartwright, Cobbett, Hunt, Wolsely and about a dozen others, which were roared with such gusto they were clearly heard a mile away in Huddersfield.[7]

This meeting was intended as part of a series of grand assemblies held throughout the country to demonstrate the people's desire for reform. The campaign was to culminate with a meeting in Manchester addressed by Henry Hunt on 16 August. Alarmed by the rapidly growing popularity of the radical movement, the loyalists worked themselves up into a lather of reaction which the authorities unleashed on the peaceful assembly in St Peter's Fields. The Manchester massacre, or Peterloo as the attack became derisively known, was a watershed for the constitutional reform movement. Radicals responded with a mixture of stunned disbelief and anger. On the night of Thursday 19 a hastily convened meeting of several thousands gathered on Almondbury Bank, addressed by an unknown speaker, thought to be from over the Pennines, who called on them to support their Lancashire bretheren and to attend a meeting the following evening prepared for any emergency. 'What?' came shouts from the crowd, 'With firearms ?' [8]

Anticipating an armed demonstration, if not a serious disturbance, Special Constables were sworn in and two troops of the 4th Dragoons and the Yeoman Cavalry were put on alert. Apparently, or not overtly at any rate, no meeting took place, but there was an unsubstantiated rumour of men drilling with pikes on Crosland Moor on 29 August. George Whitehead meanwhile was again active, and not only on his own patch. On 18 August he was in Manchester, where he tipped off the notoriously anti-radical constable Joseph Nadin to arrest John Tomlinson, of Cliffe End, near Longwood, on suspicion of being a radical delegate and 'man of bad character.' Tomlinson spent several uncomfortable nights in gaol before being discharged. Whether he was in Manchester in connection with the St Peter's Field meeting and why Whitehead should be there was not revealed.[9]

Locally, as nationally, the spirit of revenge was allowed to dissipate whilst the movement was torn by controversy between those who sought legal redress and those favouring continued mass mobilsation - with all its attendant risks of further confrontation. Although genuinely outraged by the massacre, the middle class Whigs, through their mouthpiece Edward Baines of the *Mercury*, encouraged restraint and attacked the more militant radicals. Joseph Mitchell in particular became the target for a campaign of vilification which depicted him as a willing accomplice of Oliver in 1817, and therefore still a provocateur. By implication, any persons or ideas associated with him were to be avoided, which in effect meant the Spenceans and the left of the Radical movement. By driving a wedge into the Radical ranks, the Whigs hoped that they would win over some who were prepared to compromise, not only over tactics, but also objectives. Nevertheless, only two weeks after Baines had publically denounced Mitchell at a county meeting at York, even the *Mercury* admitted that the patience of some radicals was exhausted, and that the 'clandestine collection of arms' was under way in Leeds.[10]

Huddersfield contingents attended a mass demonstration on Skircoat Common on Monday 2 October. The tense atmosphere, Radicals as well as Loyalists thinking their opponents were contemplating violence, was shown when rumour of an impending attack by soldiers almost created a panic amongst the crowd. The Huddersfield Radicals, undeterred when refused a requisition by the Constable yet again, announced a meeting for 8 November, 'to take into Consideration the late Events at Manchester and the Propriety of a Reform in the Commons House of Parliament.' Ninety signatories were added to the public notice. Among them was a Moldgreen weaver, Peter Lever, who was to emerge as one of the leaders of the coming insurrection. Around midday on the 8th, detachments flooded into Huddersfield from Almondbury, Deighton, Kirkheaton, Skelmanthorpe, Marsden and other villages and hamlets. Headed by a band which played the *Dead March* from *Saul*, *Rule Britannia* and other popular airs, the demonstration marched through the town beneath sixteen flags, caps of liberty and bunches of crepe, laurel and cypress on white wands. Joshua Hirst of Deighton carried a flag depicting a lion and the motto *'Rise Britons, Assert Reform - The British Lion Roused'*. Hirst was one who was to take this exhortation literally.

Other flags also bore menacing quotations, even those based on scriptural authority :

> *'He that hath no sword, let him sell his garment and buy one';*
> *'God armeth the Just: the Judge of all the Earth, he will do right.'*

One black banner proclaimed *'Liberty or Death'*. and Justice was shown with the text,

> *'No Corn laws; Death or Liberty; arm yourselves against Tyrants: Unite and be Free'.*

A full length figure of Henry Hunt was captioned,

> *'The Hero and Champion of Liberty - We demand the Rights of Men'.*

Verses adorned some flags :-

> *'We sigh and groan beneath the courtly train;*
> *Till our united efforts break the accursed chain.'*

A scene of the felling of a tree by John Bull and reformers was described:-

> *'The tree of corruption, the bane of our isle,*
> *By unity may be cut down,*
> *Be firm then ye Britons, the monster exile,*
> *And freedom will then be your own.'*

One flag which flew that day, still preserved in Tolson Museum, reveals the level of artistic design achieved. The Skelmanthorpe universal suffrage flag, designed by a fancy weaver, combines a reference to Peterloo with the depiction of a supplicating chained man, and the slogan of the of the Anti-slavery Society, 'Am I not a Man & Brother.' under the all-seeing eye - the symbol on the masthead of the *Manchester Observer*.

Skelmanthorpe Radical Flag, now in Tolson Museum
(Reproduced by kind permission of Kirklees Cultural Services)

And so, gaily proclaiming its objectives,the column of marchers wound its way towards Almondbury Bank. A large contingent from Halifax, including two bands, 28 flags and, symbolic of corruption, caterpillar eaten cabbages, caught up with the main body, making a crowd of over 8,000 before the hustings.
Dickinson of Dewsbury was again in the chair and, mindful of the Halifax meeting, warned them against 'false alarms' and provocation, if cavalry approached. There were no outside speakers since they were busy with other meetings and it was local men, Chris Wood and Micah Wright who presented resolutions calling for the full franchise, annual parliaments and vote by ballot and condemning the actions of the magistrates and yeomanry at Manchester. One resolution referred also to the harmful economic effects caused by taxes and 'by passing corn and combination laws to screen monopoly in machinery - which has nearly withdrawn the wealth of our country from the most useful of men, the labourers and middle tradesmen...' and condemned the Malthusian over-population theory of poverty as 'blasphemy.'

Some of the disagreements amongst the Radicals surfaced during Dickinson's summing up, when he remarked that, personally, he would be prepared to settle for less than Cartwright's Bill of Rights and accept triennial parliaments and household suffrage 'rather than create civil war.' Voices from the crowd interrupted, with cries of 'The thing and nothing but the thing!' and 'Annual Paliaments.' Assuring them that he had no intention of trying to dictate to the meeting, he reaffirmed, to cheers of approval, that he was still an advocate of the full demands. John Spivey followed with a contrasting speech, 'filled with very unmeasured abuse of all the adversaries of reform' which again the *Mercury* thought unprintable. The suggestion made by James Mann at the previous meeting, that women should become more involved, had been heeded, and Alice Tittensor, representing the female reformers of Paddock, presented Dickinson with a cap of liberty which he placed on his head, announcing that he was not ashamed to wear it. He also read out an address composed by Alice 'to her dear sisters, the female reformers of Huddersfield'.

Richard Lee then made his first, and last, recorded public appearance since his release in 1817. He began a zealous speech, saying how he had suffered for the cause of reform and, although he had not been at Manchester, he had seen blood flow in Yorkshire for the cause - a reference to Riley's suicide. 'I expect when t' boroughmongering faction meets they'll suspend t'liberties of the people. I will stand by it with my person.' A long pause followed as his mind went blank. Turning to Dickinson he said 'I'm quite puzzled', causing the whole meeting and the chairman to erupt into laughter.

Totally at a loss, Lee recovered his tongue enough to explain that he had a good deal to say when he got up, 'but somehow he had forgotten it all, however he was a friend to the cause and they should have it as it was.' Dickinson thanked him, explaining, 'his heart was so big with the subject that it had stopped his utterance.'

Dickinson then read an address cautioning them not to 'injure the cause by any rash or improper acts,' despite recent events in Manchester and Ireland, which revealed that the lower classes were regarded more as enemies than as fellow citizens by their rulers. He closed with an appeal 'to touch their pockets by soliciting a subscription on behalf of the Manchester sufferers, though,' he added mischievously, 'the custom had originated with a man whom he did not like.' Cries of, 'Name him' and replies of 'Mitchell' were shouted from several of the audience. This gave Dickinson the opportunity to launch into an attack on Mitchell's role in 1817 thereby sowing doubts in the minds of those who might be contemplating a similar venture. Hats were passed round for the collection and after a vote of thanks to Cartwright, Hunt, Cobbett, Wooller and the chairman, Dickinson closed the meeting with a reminder to abstain from taxed items, saying his own family was saving 6s. a week, and they could use a substitute for tea and 'toast and water instead of fermented liquors'.

As the crowd dispersed, no one dreamt that another decade was to pass before demands for parliamentary reform were to be raised again at a mass demonstration on Almondbury Bank. Events were to prove Richard Lee's stilted speech more astute than any polished rhetoric by Dickinson. The government did not need any provocation to crush the liberties of the people. The very fact that large numbers of workers were demanding democratic rights caused fear enough. In December the infamous 'Six Acts' were passed, which not only outlawed arming and drilling, but also curtailed the freedoms of assembly and the press. The constitutional road to reform had again led nowhere.

MELANCHOLY YORKSHIRE -
YOUR REFORMERS STAND TRUE
The Uprising of 1820

Sometime in the weeks following the Almondbury Bank meeting, a number of Huddersfield Radicals, including Joshua Hirst of Deighton (who later gave the account on which much of the evidence rests), began to meet at Joseph Pilling's house near the Red Lion to 'discuss politics and a revolution.' Some had already drawn the conclusion that 'it was no longer any use to petition parliament, but they would obtain what they wanted by physical force.' Contacts with other towns, established through the Union Societies, already existed and a report by a spy 'Alpha', although unsubstantiated, refers to delegates from Huddersfield, Paisley, Carlisle and Manchester at a meeting at Nottingham in late 1819. The first three of these towns at least were in the forefront of the developing revolutionary movement.[1]

The origins of the national organisation were revealed over two years later by Joseph Brayshaw, a Yeadon schoolmaster, in an account ostensibly intended to set the record straight, but which gave his own selective version of events, omitting vital incriminating details. Through late November and December, as the Six Acts were being passed, the Leeds Radicals prepared to go underground. Meetings began to be held secretly, often with James Mann's book shop acting as a contact point. As at Huddersfield it was concluded that reform:

'would never be obtained but by physical force and it was held out as absolutely necessary that a time should be fixed upon for the purpose of commencing revolutionary operations.'

In early 1820 Peter Lever, the Huddersfield delegate, a weaver from Moldgreen, was introduced by James Mann to Brayshaw as 'a very worthy friend of reform'. Lever, one of the more militant delegates, 'upbraided the reformers of the neighbourhood of Leeds on account of their backwardness.' He claimed, on what authority we do not know, that all the major towns south to London, those of Lancashire and Cheshire, the Newcastle area and West of Scotland were ready to rise. Brayshaw was not convinced, and in February it was decided to send delegates to assess the state of readiness in the country. Lever was assigned Lancashire and Cheshire, Mann the Midlands and London ,and Brayshaw the North. Mann returned from his mission claiming he had not made contacts at towns on the way, whilst, in the capital itself, there was no organisation except the Thistlewood group, which he had given a wide berth since it was penetrated by spies. Brayshaw doubted his enthusiasm for the task, stating in his disclosures that Thistlewood was thought to be the main organiser in London and should have been contacted, if only to warn him that Leeds was not yet prepared. There is therefore no evidence of liaison between the London revolutionaries and Yorkshire, although, according to a Huddersfield magistrate there was a local delegate, John Crowther, 'alias Balbiner...a very dangerous character,' in London in February.

Brayshaw, in the guise of a commercial traveller, visited a number of towns on his journey northwards, finding that revolutionary plans were being made only among a few colliers in the Newcastle area. Preparations had begun in Glasgow, but had been set-back by the arrest of deputies at a meeting a few days previously, although some of the Radicals remained confident. They had since sent a delegate into England. On his way home, Brayshaw found that Carlisle 'was the only place where any preparations of importance existed.' He then, for some undisclosed reason, visited Huddersfield before returning to Leeds where he met delegates from Huddersfield, Manchester and Glasgow. He gave them the discouraging report and said he could take no further part in 'encouraging revolutionary proceedings.' He was told, 'I might please myself, but they were sent to fix upon a day for a general rising, and they were determined to fix on one.' Only a few Leeds radicals arrived at a meeting to hear Brayshaw's report-back on his mission and he suspected local leaders, such as Mann, of suppressing the information. He then learned that Leeds delegates had joined others at a fateful meeting in Huddersfield and consequently:

'It was the men who met at Huddersfield on the memorable day who were the framers of the plot known by the name of the April Fool plot...'

Tom Morgan, a Barnsley weaver, also later recollected that fortnightly meetings, initially held at Leeds, were moved to Huddersfield, and that the Barnsley, Leeds, Manchester, Wakefield and Huddersfield committees maintained regular contact with each other. One of the leaders of the insurgents in Barnsley, Thomas Ferrimond, said he had once met Peter Lever in Leeds. From this and subsequent events, it would appear that the basis of Brayshaw's recollections were true. Revolutionary organisation in Yorkshire centred on the Huddersfield Radicals.

Links between the various areas testified to by Brayshaw certainly existed. John McIntyre visited Manchester in January as the Glasgow delegate and he may be the suspect from Paisley of that name who was involved in the final preparations in Huddersfield. There was also a further meeting in the vicinity of Nottingham sometime in March, attended by a Paisley delegate John Neill, and Joseph Pilling from Huddersfield, which set the date for the uprising for the night of 31 March, and the declaration of a *'Provisional Government'* the following day. A much more extensive network of revolutionaries existed than in 1817 and at a local level there was far more detailed planning. [2]

Deepening economic destitution was also fuelling discontent. At the end of January the *Mercury* reported:

> 'In Huddersfield and the populous villages by which it is surrounded, a
> very laborious investigation has been made into the condition of the poor,
> and the result has been to exhibit a picture of human misery and distress
> which has astonished those who were before well convinced that the
> labouring classes were suffering severe privations.'

By April there was still 'much real distress from want of employment' but in the
opinion of the authorities, and from the accounts of the insurgents, it is evident
that the rising was not a simple response to distress any more than it had been in
1817 or 1812. [3]

Impetus for the Huddersfield rising was also provided by smouldering
anger over the injustice of Peterloo and its aftermath. In February, the military
commander in the town reported to general Byng that a fire, at stables used by a
member of the yeomanry, was suspected arson, since the property was owned
by a Manchester man - a juror at the the whitewash inquest on John Lees, who
died of wounds inflicted at Peterloo. Whether this was in fact the motive or not,
Huddersfield magistrates considered that the 'spirit of the people in this
neighbourhood is very ripe for mischief.' The trial of Hunt, Bamford and the
other organisers of the Manchester meeting had been transferred from Lancaster
to York and, as prosecution witnesses passed through Huddersfield on 14
March, they were 'assailed with hisses groans and imprecations', whilst, in
contrast, the defendant, Dr Joseph Healey and his witnesses were given every
assistance. The trial, which returned guilty verdicts, did not finish until 27
March, that is within days of the intended rising, and served as a reminder that
Radicals could expect no redress from the legal system. When the defendants
were released on bail to await sentencing, Bamford and his party returned via
Huddersfield, where they found no one prepared to hire them the extra team of
horses, needed to draw the heavily laden carriage over Crosland Moor. The
Huddersfield Radicals again demonstrated their sympathy by harnessing
themselves to the vehicle and pulling it all the way to Blackmoor Foot. [4]

Meanwhile, despite the arrest of Arthur Thistlewood and his comrades on
23 February, which should have dispelled any hopes of support for the rising
from London, the Huddersfield committee continued preparations. Samuel
Norcliffe, a clothier, found out about the plan when he visited his uncle,
Edmund Norcliffe, at Mirfield around 9 March. John Lindley, a nailmaker, and
two others were talking with Edmund, who told Sam that soon there would be
an 'endeavour to put down the government and those who were inclined to join
in it should be getting ready with arms.' Lindley said he was Mirfield delegate
to the Huddersfield committee and they needed money to support those
delegates employed in organising the uprising. Samuel was sceptical of the
story, but was assured by Lindley that Huddersfield was in communication with
Sheffield, Barnsley, Birmingham and other places, and a man from Scotland had

attended one of the meetings. Whether or not Sam actually learned in such a casual manner what was happening, he became involved in the preparations. If his uncle is the Edmund Norcliffe who, whilst at Almondbury, was the recipient of the letter written from Mirfield by the Republican James Gledhill in 1800, then, possibly, the Norcliffes were more deeply implicated than Sam dared admit. Before the rising Edmund visited Almondbury, where one of his brothers still lived, and was told that there they had already prepared pike shafts and grenades.[5]

Around the end of February, Joseph Smith, a joiner, called at the blacksmiths shop of Joseph Barker near his home at Colne Bridge, and asked him to make a pike-head. Barker said he didn't know how, and a few days later he accompanied Smith to the house of the shoemaker, William Rainsley, where he was shown one, but not of the exact shape Smith required. A week later, Smith returned with a wooden pattern. Based on this, Barker and his step-sons Ben and George, manufactured around 17 pike-heads for 2s. each, mainly for a group of weavers from Upperheaton - Sam Ellis, Charles Drake, John Rhodes, Jonas Drake, John Stocks and Joseph France, as well as a for a collier, Sam Sharpe of Colne Bridge and Anthony Bray, a Deighton clothier. Some were also made for Rastrick men who, appropriately, as several were croppers, referred to them by the code name of 'shears'. John Lindley, of Mirfield, ordered some with screw-on heads, but it is not clear whether this was the same design as Smith's. Joseph explained to his sons they were 'for the purpose of protecting themselves when the rebellion broke out.' The Barkers had more than a business interest in pike production, since they were to join the actual rising. [6]

On 12 March, Joseph Pilling asked Joshua Hirst to meet him at Shaw's, the bookbinders, Cowmarket. When Hirst arrived, he found a delegate from Rastrick there. Pilling took them to a meeting at Berry Brow school room, where Peter Lever and delegates from different parts of the country were gathered, although Hirst does not say from how far afield. After the news was read out and discussed, it was agreed 'that they had every reason to hope that all parts of the country were getting on rapidly for a revolution and that it would shortly be affected.' Hirst was asked to prepare his people at Deighton with arms and Pilling was delegated to go to Birmingham. The following week, Sunday 19 March, Hirst again visited Shaw's to be directed to a meeting, this time at Joseph Starkey's house at Cowcliffe, where Lever, William Hirst, also from Huddersfield, Joseph Smith from Colne Bridge and about a dozen other delegates were gathered. Joshua recollected that 'the conversation at this meeting was for a general rising for the purpose of obtaining a revolution.' An official signal for the rising had been devised to ensure that it happened simultaneously and only on the go ahead of the Committee. Peter Lever had prepared cards with *'Democracy'* written on them. These were then cut into two, and half given to each of the delegates, who were instructed to await a messenger with the matching half and then mobilise their men. On 26 March delegates, 'the greater part of whom had been military men', met again at Cowcliffe, when 'Peter Lever called them together for the purpose of concerting a plan for attacking the town of Huddersfield.' Jackson of Moldgreen wrote the plan down, which was taken by William Hirst to be scrutinised by other members of the Huddersfield committee. Final preparations were to be made on Thursday, 30 March, the day before the uprising.

John Lindley returned to Mirfield, calling at the Norcliffes' where he met Daniel Micklethwaite, John Peacock, John Winter and a carpenter called Wynn. John Tyas of Rastrick was also present. Someone said they needed money for gun powder to make cartridges and they should subscribe 6d each. Tyas refused, saying 'Where the devil was he to get 6d.' Samuel Norcliffe asked how they were to be sure a general rising was to take place and that they would not be deceived. Lindley explained about the *'Democracy'* cards, assuring them that the signal would be genuine. On the day before the rising Sam went to Peacock's house and found James Hemingway and an old man in an upstairs chamber making ball cartridges. 'I think you're throng' he commented. 'Yes we are,' one replied 'we have made between five or six pounds and we want three pounds weight more [of powder] to make up all the balls we have.' Whether Sam had come to help he did not later reveal, but he took six cartridges home which, he claimed, his mother destroyed, refusing to have 'none suchlike things in the house.'

Unlike 1817, the Yorkshire authorities apparently had no inkling of what was going on, so efficient had the revolutionaries been in preserving their clandestinity. Almost at the last minute, the plan came near to being exposed. A package arrived in Huddersfield on the Regulator coach from Birmingham on 30 March, addressed to John Payne, Castlegate. Someone noticed an object sticking out, which was revealed to be the point of a bayonet. George Whitehead waited at the coach office and arrested a cropper, John Gill, when he came to collect it. Gill, although he was reputed to be a 'notorious radical', claimed he was only picking it up for Payne and didn't know its contents. Inside, along with an invoice for sale of the goods at half price, were 3 bayonets at 14d., 2 brace of pistols at 16s per brace, 2 gunlocks at 14d each and 2 bullet moulds for both pistol and musket ammunition at 4d each. Gill was released and after the rising went on the run.[7]

Around 20 delegates attended the final Cowcliffe meeting. As well as Lever, Jackson, Joshua Hirst, and William Hirst, there were men from Berry Brow, Honley, Marsden, Lindley, Elland, Rastrick, Ripponden and Liversedge. A delegate from Glasgow had also arrived. Lever outlined the situation. 'The whole country was ready for revolution'. Manchester, Leeds, Wakefield,

Barnsley, Sheffield and Glasgow were fully prepared. The plan was to march on Huddersfield and, if resistance was shown by the military and magistrates, to give battle. Mirfield and Ripponden were each to provide about 1000 men, and large numbers were expected from Elland, Rastrick, Brighouse, Netheroyd Hill and Cowcliffe to the west and north of the town, and a further thousand from Skelmanthorpe, Heaton, Almondbury, Moldgreen and Dalton to the south and east. Each division was to assemble about a mile and a quarter from the town centre. The signal to attack would be the lighting of a beacon on Castle Hill, the ancient hill-fort which had been part of the invasion signal system during the war with France. Those attacking from the upper end of the town were to take on the cavalry, the Skelmanthorpe and Mirfield men the infantry, and the Huddersfield men themselves would seize the magistrates quarters at the George Inn. 'When they were in possession of the town they would establish a free government or a government by the people and they were to provide for the families by issuing out notes.' The success of the rising was to be signalled by the stopping of the coaches. Lever then left the meeting on a mission to Halifax. Joshua Hirst recollected seeing him mount a horse for the journey. The Scottish delegate, (whom the magistrates later identified as James McIntyre, a Paisley weaver, five foot ten to eleven inches tall, with dark hair, whiskers and a long, pale visage), attempted to write down the places referred to, but was unable to spell the unfamiliar Yorkshire names. Tempest Tiffany, the Rastrick delegate and ex-Luddite, wrote them down for him.

At some point, either in this meeting, or soon afterwards, a severe disagreement arose with the delegates representing Berry Brow, Honley and Holmfirth. They refused to be involved in a night attack, saying that it should be done by day, and, if Huddersfield was successfully captured, they were ready to join in the following morning . Whether any of these men had learned by direct experience of the 1817 failure is not revealed, but they apparently favoured an attack in the light of day when any military disadvantage would be compensated for by popular support. The *Mercury* was to comment on the absence of activity in the Holme and Colne Valleys, but put a slightly cynical interpretation on the attitude of those Radicals - 'they would wait till the next morning to see how the new government got on.'[8]

As expected, the signal came on Friday 31 March. Reportedly, word was brought by a man from Manchester who arrived by coach and went immediately to Cowcliffe from where, by evening, around twenty messengers were dispatched with the halves of the *'Democracy'* cards for the local leaders. According to the *Mercury* it was already apparent that something was in the wind

'**A very unusual sensation was observed in many of the villages in the neighbourhood of Huddersfield towards the evening of Friday 31st. The**

**women were seen passing about to each other's houses, many of them in
tears, and several of the men appeared unsettled, as if meditating some
daring enterprise.'**

At Colne Bridge, 'unsettled' was something of an understatement. The
Barkers were kept busy almost up to the last minute. Most of the pike-heads
were completed, and had been collected the night before. Joseph Smith brought
a shaft which Ben Barker fixed to the head for him. Only a few days before,
Barker senior had complained about late orders when Joseph Tyas delivered a
pattern for a pike head, drawn by Joseph Fallas of Rastrick. Tyas was called out
of his house on Friday morning by Ben Wrigley, who told him that the
revolution was to begin that night, and he was to get ready without telling his
wife. Tyas complained that he wasn't well, and appeared so unenthusiastic that
Tempest Tiffany called round and asked 'Hast thou given over working for a
revolution.' Joseph assured him he hadn't and 'Tiff' recounted the plan to
advance on Huddersfield in four divisions. The Rastrick men were to assemble
in Grimescar Wood and the attack was to be signalled by a rocket from
Cowcliffe. Later Fallas, along with Wrigley and Jonathan Brook, came to ask
Tyas to fetch the pike from Barker. He was given the 2s. to pay for it, and since
it was wet and by now he was obviously poorly, Fallas loaned him a top-coat.
About four o'clock he arrived at Barkers' smithy and found the two step-sons
forging pikes while two young lads turned the grindstone to finish them. He
told them that that night 'there was going to be a stir,' and outlined the plan
described by Tiff.

Joseph Smith later arrived with the **'*Democracy*'** card complete and told
the Barkers, Charles Crosland, a spinner, and James Taylor, a mason, that 'there
will be a general rising that night and they might be getting ready by half-past
ten to go to Huddersfield'. They were expecting 15,000 to rise on all sides of
the town, and the Colne Bridge detachment was to assemble at Whitacre's Mill,
near the canal at Deighton, until they saw the signal rocket from Castle Hill. He
also brought a pistol which needed cleaning. That was not the last request that
evening. Nathaniel Buckley, a clothier from Ledger Bridge, turned up with an
old file for conversion into a pike head. Joseph Barker told him he had given
up work for the day and left his sons to make one out of material from the
workshop, the file being unsuitable. It was almost eleven when Ben and
George left the smithy for the house.

There they found their father with James Taylor, Tom Barlow and
William Rainsley, who also had a gun which needed mending. It was not until
twelve that George had done the repairs, during which time two other men came
to fetch pikes. Together they left the house and climbed the hill out of Colne
Bridge to the house of Mark Brook, a mason, but he refused either to join them
or give up his gun. After this inauspicious start they joined Joseph Smith,

Charles Crosland and Sam Sharpe. George Barker and Rainsley went into a field where they found about ten men assembled. Sam and Joseph Ellis, John Stocks, Frank Dransfield, William Tyas and Joseph France were all armed with pikes. Paul Kaye had a large pistol. Tom France and James Brook had no weapons at all, having applied too late for pikes. At least three others joined the body as they marched off along the canal bank towards Huddersfield.

Meanwhile at Knowle, Mirfield, Edmund Norcliffe and John Lindley were busy much of the day splitting ash poles for shafts and straightening scythe blades in the fire for pike heads. The hammering was heard by a neighbour Hannah Schofield, whose curiosity had already been aroused by the comings and goings of strangers at the Norcliffes' house, particularly on Sundays. At about eight o'clock, a young man arrived from Huddersfield with the matching half of Lindley's signal card. The stranger said they were to make their way to Bradley Mill Lane end by half past twelve and join contingents from Dalton, Deighton and elsewhere. The object was to disarm the soldiers and take control of the town. They were to remain disciplined, since they would 'make a law that the first found plundering was to be shot.' Lindley asked Sam Norcliffe to go and tell the men to get ready as soon as possible. He called on Peacock, who said he would mobilise his men, and then went to Lee Green, where he told several people, 'It seems the Revolution is to begin this evening.' Crossing some fields he arrived on the turn-pike road and again met-up with Lindley at the blacksmith's shop of Joseph Holmes. Holmes refused to go with them to Huddersfield, saying they would all be killed, and his wife, Fanny, persuaded him to come indoors. Peacock, Buckley and George Crabtree arrived equipped with pikes, William Hill and George Hirst carried scythes, and only William Illingworth and John Winter had guns. They returned to Knowle and found that Edmund had gone to bed. Apparently, they had not expected him to accompany them. Pikes were fetched out of the mistal and reared up against the house wall to equip those who arrived without weapons. Hannah Schofield, from her stables, saw about a dozen of them, one having a large blade with a hook. Lindley and another, at ten to eleven, went to the *Kings Head* in Cripplegate, where the talk was already of revolution and persuaded Tom, George, Sam and James Gill to accompany him to Knowle. Hannah Schofield had meanwhile retired to bed, but between eleven and twelve was disturbed by noise. Peeping out of the window she saw about a score of men 'with spears' and heard Sam Norcliffe say 'Go form in abreast lads' before they marched out. She also recollected 'I saw Edmund Norcliffe's two little daughters follow them to see them off.'

Joseph Tyas had returned to Rastrick and delivered the pike to Fallas before going home. Jonathan Brook arrived about nine to ask if he was ready. He answered that he was too ill to be of any use, to which Brook replied helpfully, 'He might ride on a baggage waggon if there was any.' Unconvinced of the practicality of this suggestion, Tyas went to bed. About this time, William Halstead, a Rastrick manufacturer, ventured into the road 'where there were a number of children and women standing, talking about a general rising of the people which they said was to take place that night.' Over the next few hours a large number of men and women had collected and eventually, after an argument about whether to go straight to Huddersfield or via Brighouse, the men were organised into some sort of order and marched off. Halstead stayed discreetly in a field to avoid being 'impressed' to join. For some reason Tiffany led a separate party of 15 men while a larger group, headed by Henry Wrigley and Henry Lee, went to Fixby Park, where at least 50 men of the northern division were assembled.

At Fixby, sometime after midnight, John Mitchell, a butcher, heard a rattling at the door. A voice said they could not wait for him, but must have his arms directly since - 'the drums and bugles are going at Huddersfield and we cannot stop'. Opening the door, two men whom he recognised, George Firth and Job Barker of Birchencliffe, and another man, each with a pike, entered and asked him to fetch his gun. He complied. He knew both Firth and Barker to be radicals, and he had 'no doubt they took his gun to stand against the soldiers.' Joseph Tiffany, a cropper at Cowcliffe, was alerted by a neighbour, Charlotte Nutter, who told him there were a number of men in Fixby Park. He estimated there were around 300, and later they were joined by a few others from Rastrick. After midnight he returned home, but later 'perceiving the neighbours so much out of their houses I went out again.' But then the moon clouded over and little was to be seen.[9]

It was at Lindley where there was the most determined attempt to raid for arms, Luddite fashion. About five in the afternoon John Wilson, a cropper, was called into the house of another cropper, David Hepworth and was told by his wife 'she had been informed there was going to be a rise that night.' That evening he saw two men he knew acting suspiciously, one coming out of a fold with a long stick with a coat over it, and another who fired a pistol in the air. He also heard other shots fired off around Lindley. Richard Fox, cropper, heard a violent knocking on his door sometime before midnight and a 'Hello'. He asked what they wanted. 'Open the door. We are come for your gun. You must either deliver it or come yourself.' He opened the door and was confronted by about twenty men. It was moonlight and he 'could see the pikes glitter very fairly.' John Waterhouse, a farmer was woken at twenty past twelve by his daughter who told him 'the revolution had begun.' Through the chamber window he could see 20 to 30 men in front of the house with long sticks. A violent knocking and a demand for arms came from the back of the house. He hurriedly took his gun from its hook and hid it upstairs. Three men, one with a hayfork and two with pikes, were admitted by his wife. They said he must either go with them or hand over his gun. His wife fetched it for them and they promised it would be returned. He thought he recognised George Pilling, a Birchencliffe cropper amongst them. Tom Wilkinson, a cropper, when he heard the demand for his gun took it from the balks (beam) and, so he said, put it outside the door without looking. At the house of the carpenter, John Ellam, the insurgents knew that his lodger Charles Firth owned a gun and asked for either the weapon or its owner to accompany them. Tom Rhodes, cropper, Tom Schofield, master cropper of Marsh and Job Barker of Birchencliffe were identified as those guarding the door.

Elizabeth, wife of Ben Milnes, an innkeeper, was alarmed by a large number of men at the door at about half past eleven. Her lodger, Joseph Firth, and a servant, Alice Garside, were up sitting by the fire. Alice opened the door and about 20 men armed with pikes entered and demanded Firth's gun. He handed it over but it had no lock. About a hour later, after they had gone to bed, she heard knocking again and raised the sash to call out of the window that they had no gun. 'We demand some ale', replied someone 'It's not a gun we want, thou must look pretty sharp.' She opened the door and the men, realising she was afraid, said they would stand outside in the 'towngate'. She left a gallon of ale near the door, which was taken out by a very tall man with a white apron. They wouldn't let her shut the door until another gallon was drawn and then they departed, leaving the pitcher and glass. She didn't ask them to pay. Meanwhile, John Wilson had secreted himself in a hay loft which overlooked the Huddersfield road. Around midnight he saw about 100 men with long sticks over their shoulders, he wasn't sure (or wouldn't say) whether they had pike heads on. The men were ordered into three companies. As the first passed by he heard someone complain ' "They are all badly in bed when they should come forwards, but we will stand to a man or die to a man," or some such expression'.

Men of the proposed southern division had also taken up arms and made for Amondbury Bank, where the forces were to be mustered. At ten to one the toll-gate keeper at Dogley Lane, Jonathan Parrot, saw several men from the direction of Kirkburton pass through the gate towards Huddersfield. Over an hour later he was awoken by a company of men estimated at 100 strong. John Hardcastle the younger, a Kirkburton fancy weaver, also encountered fifty men at Dogley Bar Toll in three companies, ten yards apart. Further on he met another fifty. They all appeared to have been drilled. What he himself was doing on the road so late he didn't explain. At Almondbury the rising seems less organised. The only witness was Marmaduke Ranson, a coachman, who, around one o'clock, saw two persons 'running backwards and forwards in the streets'. An hour later he saw a number of people march pass his window towards Huddersfield. Two or three had pikes and some had guns sloped over their shoulders and were wearing white hats, the radical symbol. At least twenty shots were fired into the night sky.

Joshua Hirst had received his half of the *'Democracy'* card about seven. He informed 'his people' and, equipped with a gun and ammunition, led the others armed with pikes to Bradley Mill. Only about a dozen others arrived at the rendezvous. They waited in vain for the great force which was expected. Hirst despondently concluded it was another 'Oliver job', and made his way home.

After they had left Norcliffe's house the Mirfield men proceeded via Wasps Nest to Battyeford, where they were joined by Sam Hirst, and on to Dumb Steeple at Cooper Bridge, the site of the rendezvous for the attack on Rawfolds mill in 1812. Ben Armitage of Clifton met up with them. He had tried to demand a gun at the house of Tom Crabtree, a gardener, at Hartshead, but being told there was no firearm in the house grabbed a large pair of garden shears. Crabtree's wife snatched them back and he came away empty handed. While the revolutionaries were waiting at Dumb Steeple for the anticipated reinforcements they were encountered by a group of men on the way home from the *Horseshoes* at the bottom of Mirfield Moor. Robert Tolson junior, a fancy manufacturer from Dalton, and John Hinchliffe a Bradley farmer, had been warned by the landlady of strange persons moving about, and had decided to go home together. They were joined by a gamekeeper from Cooper Bridge and two other men from Brighouse and Clifton. At the 'weighing machine', near the Steeple, they saw a circle of unarmed men, and Hinchliffe was rash enough to ask what they were doing and to order them to disperse saying 'Are you going to murder, or what are you for.' Tolson, to avoid trouble, advised him to 'let them alone. They are only a few lads met together.' But then the Brighouse man noticed the pikes stacked under the wall and picked one up. An insurgent grabbed it from him, cutting his hand, and a brief melee followed. Hinchliffe seized a pike, and other men who had been out of sight in the field jumped over the wall. Both Hinchliffe and Tolson were struck with pike staffs and Tolson was jabbed in the back. As they made a hasty retreat some one said 'Fire an alarm,' and a shot was discharged which Hinchliffe swore whizzed past his ear.

This skirmish proved too much for at least two of the rebels who refused to march any further. Sam Norcliffe himself said he only went as far as Bradley Bar then returned home. It was a much diminished force which continued on to Bradley Mill Lane End, led by Lindley. They found no one there. Joshua Hirst and the Deighton men must have already dispersed. Lindley's party turned back along the footpath and met the Colne Bridge men coming from Whitacre's Mill. 'Huddersfield was quieter than it had been for a day or two,' Lindley told them in disgust. The Barkers and a couple of others decided to call it a night, while the others remained for about a quarter of an hour hoping for some sign that the revolution was still in progress.

The last rebels to remain under arms were those of the western division, where the Lindley men, reinforced by others from Ripponden and Barkisland, made a force which reports put at several hundred strong. At least an advance party reached Greenhead, where they halted opposite Trinity Church, recently built by the magistrate, B. H. Allen, and drew up across the road in ranks six deep. They apparently had a determination and a confidence in numbers lacking in the other divisions, as it 'was only the earnest entreaty of their leaders which prevented them making their attack, though informed the others had not done it.'

John Whitacre, the merchant and millowner, was on the look-out for any trouble. One of his workers, Ben Heywood, had warned him 'there was to be a rising of Reformers that night and they were going to attack the town of Huddersfield, a great part of the men in Deighton, where he lived, were arming themselves with scythes, pitchforks, guns and bayonets. A great many balls had been cast... as would fill two strikes.' At around two, Whitacre was gazing towards Castle Hill when he saw a light 'resembling a beacon or a balloon.' A few minutes later a series of shots were heard from Dalton, Almondbury, Cowcliffe and Marsh areas. Robert Tolson meanwhile, still bleeding, called on Tom Kilner, a bailiff at Dalton. As Tolson was being helped to the house of Thomas Atkinson of Bradley Mill, commander of the Yeomanry, where his wound was dressed, Kilner went out over Dalton Bank. He saw, in the moonlight, a group of men marching in regular order towards Colne Bridge. One urged the others 'Be steady.' Over the following two hours he heard at least 150 shots. Richard Thornton, a dyer of Dalton Green, was awake from twelve, when ten armed men had come to demand his gun, until three. He also heard firing continue well into the night. According to the *Mercury* other witnesses had seen rockets go up before the signal beacon was lit.

The Huddersfield magistrates had meanwhile established their headquarters in the George Hotel. The Yeomanry had been mobilised and, along with a troop of the 4th Dragoon Guards and three companies of the 85th Regiment of Foot, remained on alert all night, awaiting the anticipated attack. In the morning patrols were sent out to reconnoitre, but they saw no sign of the rebels. Over the following days a few arms were recovered, including scythes and pikes with screw-heads about nine inches long. In Almondbury some weapons were recovered, along with a stock of pike staves which had been cut from ash plantations. Arrests began. The Barkers, Lindley, Peacock, Nat Buckley and Joshua Hirst were among the first batch, charged with 'being under arms.'

Several others went on the run, including, Lever, Pilling and Gill. One of them, a gardener, James Wilson, went to Barnsley where he told committee men that he had broken into the house of his master with a gavelock and stolen a gun. He assured them that the movement had not been defeated and 'was sure the Huddersfield people would make some agreement to rise at some future time which would be agreed on Easter Monday.' Signs that rank and file radicals had certainly abandoned ideas of further action is evident from their return of guns which had been borrowed. Wilkinson of Lindley found his reared up outside his door on the morning after the rising. Someone tried to put John Waterhouse's gun inside his door but the door catch was fast. A voice said 'Here is your piece, thankyou sir.' When Waterhouse went out it was leaning against the wall with a new flint fitted. The gun of Mitchell of Fixby also had a new flint when a man returned it saying 'I have brought the gun back and I hope there is no offence.' Richard Thornton of Dalton found his on Monday morning when he went to his work at Senior & Beaumont's dyehouse. Although some of these witnesses may have willingly loaned their guns to the rebels, the conscientiousness with which they were returned is not the behaviour of men who were intent, in the words of the magistrates, 'to rob and plunder.'

But other incidents gave the authorities cause to think that rebellion had not ended. On Sunday 2 April a body of around 40 men was encountered by Tom Swift, a fine drawer, as he was riding along the Thornhill to Whiteley road. One attempted to slash his bridle with a pike as he spurred past, and the blade cut his trousers. Two days later, as the Yeomanry rode through the streets of Huddersfield, they were hissed at by the populace and the 'town for some time wore an alarming aspect.' A Honley man, who was thought to be a ringleader, was chased into a tobacconists by the Yeomanry and arrested. The magistrates convened a meeting on Wednesday evening and reported to around 100 of the town's principal inhabitants that between 1600 and 2000 insurgents had been under arms the previous Friday 'whose object it was to change by force the existing order of society.' An Armed Association, a middle class militia, was established with about 50 members under the command of Captain Lewis Fenton. [10]

Meanwhile Richard Addy from Barnsley had returned with Wilson in order to make contact with the Huddersfield committee but 'the people were in such a disturbed state, and the soldiers there, so that he could not get his business done.' He met some men who promised to convene a secret meeting of the committee and let Barnsley know their decision in a day or two. Although any hope of success of the revolution should have been dispelled by the defeat of a general strike in Scotland in support of the Provisional Government on 1 April, and uncoordinated risings which culminated in a shoot-out between a group of weavers and soldiers at Bonnymuir on Thursday 6th, some of the Huddersfield men clung to the hope of a further effort in Yorkshire. It was mainly on their assurances that the Barnsley Radicals continued with their plans.

On Saturday 8th a man visited Tom Morgan, a weaver, to ask to see the committee. Morgan fetched Richard Addy and James Lowe, and the latter went with the messenger to a 'field near Huddersfield.' Lowe returned on Sunday with the news he 'had met about thirty delegates from different towns and they had all agreed to meet on Grange Moor by daybreak on Wednesday morning.'[11]

Two Barnsley committee men, Stephen Kitchener and Craven Cookson, a former Luddite twister-in, visited Huddersfield on Monday evening and returned believing everything to be 'genuine'. As planned, the rising went ahead on the evening of the following day. Around two to three hundred insurgents under William Comstive, a man in his late twenties, who had fought at Waterloo as a sergeant in the the 29th Regiment of Foot, marched through the night from Barnsley and its surrounding villages to Grange Moor. They awaited daybreak and the arrival of a great Radical army from northern England and Scotland, 50,000 strong. At least one Huddersfield man and another stranger met them on Grange Moor and urged patience - 'they were sure the people from Huddersfield would come to join us.' Comstive, and his leiutenant Richard Addy, who had served in a Rifle Corps at Waterloo, discussed going to Huddersfield to find out what had happened. A group of gentlemen encountered the insurgents near Flockton at about five and galloped to alert the magistrates in Huddersfield. In the meantime news had already reached the town and barricades had been hastily thrown up around the Market Place to protect the George Inn HQ. A dawn cavalry patrol was sent out composed of ten 4th Dragoons and 16 Yeomanry. The Moor was deserted apart from the debris of the retreated army. The Yeomanry returned in triumph with their trophies - pikes and pitchforks, a drum and a 'revolutionary standard', as the *Mercury* referred to the black-fringed, green flag adorned with the biblical quote adopted as a slogan after Peterloo *'He that smiteth a Man so that he die, shall surely be put to death.*'[12]

On Friday Joseph Tyas of Rastrick was 'taken-up' and examined before the magistrates. A letter was found in his possession intended for dispatch via a carrier to Shude Hill, Manchester. It confirms both that direct contact with Manchester was maintained and that some Huddersfield Radicals really believed a general rising had been planned for the 12th, and even entertained hopes of a further attempt, concluding 'I hope that we all meet in one Body and one Voice yet...'. Its description of the abortive march to Grange Moor forms a suitably moving epitaph to the failed revolution of 1820.

> **'our bretheren in Lankaster Shire   Dearly beloved,**
> **We hope you are comeng on pretty well though your Captifeity is painful...**
> **Our Musick in Yorkshire as played twise where yours in Lankashire has**
> **never struck at all, is your Musicians sick ?... Melancholy, Melancholy,**
> **Melancholy Yorkshire, your Reformers stand true....it would have took an**
> **affect on your feelings to have seen the brave men stand under arms all**
> **that wet night after a march of 12 miles and not one man to meet them**

according to appointment. All their pike shafts were left on the moor, the blades taken out except three or four which was too fast in. The poor men stood with cheerful hearts till daylight beating the drums and their breasts but no other party joined them. All at a loss what to know what to do. Return to Barnsley they could not think of, but when there was no other prospect they all began to shed tears most bitterly with cries of the most distracted...'[13]

Although more men were involved in the 1820 rising than in 1817, and more names were known to the authorities, there were relatively far fewer arrests. Of those apprehended some like the Barkers, Joshua Hirst and Joseph Tyas named names, and never even came to trial. Only four Huddersfield men were committed to York assizes compared to nearly 20 from Barnsley. Of 62 men known to have been involved in the 1st of April rising, the occupations of 29 are known - 8 weavers, 3 clothiers, 4 croppers, 4 blacksmiths, 2 spinners, a joiner, a carpenter, a nailmaker, a cardmaker, a mason, a shoemaker, a gardener and a collier. Although, as in 1817, Huddersfield rose-up first and rose alone, links with other areas were more firmly established in 1820. The press again attributed a leading role to spies and agent provocateurs, but none were identified, and the surviving magistrates' and Home Office papers reveal no evidence of any in Yorkshire at least. One of the mysterious men with Lancashire accents identified as a spy by the *Wakefield Journal*, turned out to be the weaver John Lancashire from Middleton, a former 'Ardwick conspirator' gaoled in 1817, now living in Almondbury. He wrote to the *Mercury* to deny the accusations but obviously did not elaborate on any involvement he may have had in the rising. If there is a shadowy character it is the gardener James Wilson, who, after the 1 April rising, fled to Barnsley and encouraged the Reformers there to rise. After the failure of 12 April he later turned up in Carlisle urging a further attempt, and claiming a Provisional Government was to be established in Huddersfield! If he was a spy, it was not known to the magistrate B. H. Allen, who investigated his role and found he had indeed visited Carlisle and frequently went there, and to Scotland. He must have had means of financial support since he sometimes travelled by coach.

Allen dismissed the idea of a Provisional Government being planned in Huddersfield, but he continued to receive reports of the movement of delegates. On 10 May delegates from Nottingham, Paisley and Glasgow were supposed to be in the town, and he feared that the fugitives Lever, Pilling (who was reported to have visited Nottingham), Gill and James Hirst, still posed a threat.

'It would be most desirable if the Huddersfield Committee could be brought to justice, they are men who have been leaders in the former disturbance and I fear will always continue plotting until examples are made of them.'[14]

Huddersfield remained tense for a while. On Wednesday 13 April 'great alarm' was caused by a large explosion which turned out to be the accidental detonation of 240 rounds of ball cartridge in the infantry barracks, injuring a sergeant. A few days later a couple of pot-shots were fired into the George Inn. The culprit was found to be a member of the Yeomanry 'temporarily deranged' by his arduous duty of suppressing rebels. Bonfires on a hillside and the strains of 'Radical pipes' on the night of Tuesday 9 May caused a further alert, but it was revealed a few days later that the Radical army was in fact a group of apprentices celebrating a traditional ritual of 'burying his Old Wife'. Just over a week later the detachment of the 85th Regiment of Foot left Huddersfield, accompanied by 16 local girls who had struck up affairs with the soldiers. One, Letitia Bedford, who was prevented from going with her lover, hanged herself, an incident according to the *Mercury*, illustrative of the 'Demoralizing effects of standing armies.' No doubt the respectable citizens of Huddersfield thought it a small price to pay to save their lives and property from revolution.[15]

In September the Huddersfield and Barnsley insurgents indicted for High Treason appeared at York Assizes. With the grim example of the execution and beheading of Thistlewood and his four comrades on 1 May, it is not suprising that many should have shown contrition and remorse to the point of trying to save their own necks at the risk of others. All pleaded guilty on the understanding that their lives would be spared and formal death sentences were commuted to 14 years transportation. Some of the Barnsley rebels suffered the full term, but softened by the concession of being allowed to take their families with them. Others were released early. Lindley, Buckley and Peacock survived two years in the squalid hulks at Sheerness, until in 1822, they were taken to Woolwich and given expenses to make their way home to Huddersfield.[16]

The authorities in the town meanwhile, sought some recompense for their sacrifices in putting down rebellion. The foot barracks established in December 1819 had been funded by wealthy individuals to the tune of £500. The annual rent was £60 and that of the cavalry barracks £45.5s. B. H. Allen wrote to General Byng asking for government assistance with costs, since the inhabitants had also raised two troops of Yeoman Cavalry 'at considerable expense,' as well as equipping an Armed Association. 'We believe that no town has exerted itself more to resist the disaffected,' he pleaded. Byng supported the request, pointing out to the Home Office the town's strategic importance for controlling the manufacturing districts, 'Huddersfield from its locality is rather a desirable situation for a troop of cavalry.'[17]

MAY REVOLUTIONS NEVER CEASE
Richard Carlile and the Republican Movement 1821-1823

The Yorkshire trials attracted little attention, reflecting the general malaise affecting the Reform movement. The insurrectionists had been cowed by the supression of the revolution, whilst the main champion of the mass movement, Hunt, and several of his leading northern supporters, were in gaol. The field was left open to the middle class reformers who nailed their standard to the popular cause of Queen Caroline in her divorce dispute with George IV. Even dedicated Republicans saw the Caroline Affair as a stick with which to beat the King and his ministers. Richard Carlile, the London tinsmith gaoled in 1819 for publishing the works of Tom Paine, wrote in his popular periodical the *Republican:*

'At home the persecution of the Queen has been of great assistance to the cause of Reform, it has united all classes of reformers and in the person of the Queen our liberties seem to be for the moment centred. It has above all things shewn us the inadequacy of the present system and the impropriety of suffering it to continue.' [1]

In Marsden, the Queen's acquittal was greeted with great rejoicing. Bells rang out at the factories and Taylors' foundry. A notorious local Radical, 'Dutch' Harry Broadbent, of the Two Dutchmen Inn, insisted on ringing the church bell and, adorned in his Radical white hat, pestered the curate Abraham Horsfall, (brother of the Luddite's victim, William) until he was arrested, earning the distinction of being the last man to be placed in Marsden town stocks. The foundry owners, Enoch and James Taylor, and their partner, the skilled engineer Arthur Hirst, were not only staunch supporters of the Queen but had also belonged to a 'Wisdom Seeking Society,' along with the innovative Farnley Tyas manufacturer John Nowell, Michael Harrison of Crosland Factory and others from as far afield as Stockport and Manchester. These had begun meeting around 1812 in an isolated pub on Standedge Moor - a venue which contributed to their local reputation as 'Jacobins', although Nowell later denied that the society had any political objective being solely concerned with the discussion of scientific and technical subjects. Whatever the truth of this, the Taylors certainly had Radical connexions. Their brother George had left for America around 1800 to escape persecution for his Republican sympathies. His son Robert and the son of James Taylor, James Jnr, were to join the relatively numerous Marsden supporters of Richard Carlile who certainly did combine rationalist, scientific enquiry with revolutionary political ideas. The Taylors' atheism too was so notorious, that one local preacher caused a furore after Enoch's death by suggesting that now he was in hell making castings for the devil.[2]

Forwarding a collection of £12.0s.3d to Carlile in January 1822, Abel Hellawell, a tinplate worker from Huddersfield, described the friends at Marsden as 'most hearty in your cause'. They apparently included some wealthy ones too, since three donors, one with the alias 'Free Thinker' sent £1 each, well over an average week's wage for a worker. We may speculate whether these were the senior members of the Taylor firm. James Taylor, with his name latinised to Jacobus, and Robert were included in the list of 39 subscribers from the village. However, not all of these can be presumed to be republican and atheist sympathisers of Carlile, since, (unless this is another of Harry Broadbent's jokes), the name of the curate Abraham Horsfall DD appears. Henry Broadbent himself is listed among subscribers in September with a donation of 6d. Considering that, in a later list, the name of Carlile's local Methodist adversary, Tom Shepherd, appears alongside a donation of 3s. and the quote 'if thine enemy hunger give him meat,' there may be others who objected to the sentence, but did not condone the beliefs which had incurred it. But it is evident from many of the pseudonymns and comments that the donors *were* adherents of the politics and philosophy advocated in the *Republican*. After the first list totalling 103 names from Huddersfield, Almondbury and Marsden, Hellawell sent over 142 in September, including more than 40 from Rastrick;

'An Atheist...A Materialist...A Friend to Liberty...An Enemy to Tyranny and Oppression...A Radical Reformer...A Little Radical...A Deist' appear, along with others more witty and cryptic. In a later list Robert Taylor describes himself as 'son of an exiled Radical,' directly linking his generation with the Republicans of Paine's time. 'Old Sam Buckley,' on the Almondbury list, may be the superintendent of the United Britons committee of that name in 1802. He also appears next to an Edward Harling, the same name as the informer of 1802 who appeared to have inside information about the UB, and who may have been a sympathiser. Thomas Vevers and John Buckley are among the subscribers, both of whom were implicated in the 1817 rising. Buckley, unchastened by having given evidence against Tom Riley, and still suffering from verbal incontinence, describes himself as 'a Republican of Longroyd Bridge, a detester of Priestcraft from the high church dignatory to the smooth-faced hypocritical canting "do put some money in the plate" Methodist Parson, in short a real disciple of Mirabeaud'. Ben Hepponstale could also be the friend of Riley's who acted as a delegate in 1817. William Cottriel is presumably the framework knitter who signed the public notice of the meeting to establish a National Union Society in August 1819, whilst Matthew Vickerman and Thomas Bagshaw (a hatter) were among those calling the Almondbury Bank meeting to protest at the Manchester massacre. Micah Wright, 'once a Fanatic and now a Materialist,' moved a resolution on that occasion and John Spivey is probably the same man who made 'an intemperate speech.' Several other names coincide with those of known radicals but are too commonplace for certain identification. What is clear is that most of the remaining active, thinking, working class radicals in the Huddersfield area rallied around Richard Carlile and his *Republican*.[3]

Whether the organisation in Huddersfield bore the title Zetetic Society, adopted by bodies in other areas is not recorded, but there certainly was a society of some sort established to promote the ideas of Tom Paine. The highlight of its calendar was the celebration of Paine's birthday on 29 January. In 1823 it was chaired by Micah Wright and addressed by John Penny. Toasts, interspersed with songs, included as well as the obvious ones to Tom Paine, and his successor, Carlile - the South American republicans (now engaged in a fierce struggle with the Spanish empire), 'and may Europe follow their example'; the Spanish republicans; Mr Drakard, editor of the *Stamford News*; 'the real author of the *Systeme de la Nature*' (Mirabaud); the veteran Radicals, Muir, Palmer, Cobbett, Wooler and Hunt and 'The Republicans, Materialists and Deists of the whole kingdom.' One macabre toast referred to the suicide of the Foreign Secretary, 'May every tyrant be possessed of a white-hafted penknife, and have courage to use it in a Castlereagh form' and another encapsulated the Republican political creed

> **'May revolutions never cease while tyranny exists:**
> **May every animated being breathe the pure air of freedom and truth.'**

Abel Hellawell chaired the following years celebrations when 'The Immortal Memory of P. B. Shelley, the author of *Queen Mab*', and Horne Took, Volney and Voltaire were added to the pantheon of revered thinkers.[4]

Carlile and his followers spent much of their time and energy, not in political propagandising and organisation, but in philosophical and scientific polemics to substantiate the materialist view of the universe. Their immediate adversaries were those who upheld the superstitions of the Christian religion, and two of the most vocal were from Huddersfield, a Methodist heald and slay maker, Tom Shepherd, and James Humphreys of Springdale. In the course of his disputes with these and other critics Carlile elaborated a theory of dialectical materialism, (the concept that the basis of all existence is matter in motion and that there is no need to invoke a creator), which reveals him as the leading British working class philosopher of the nineteenth century. Because his popularity was so brief, and barely survived his release from gaol in 1825, his role has been greatly neglected. Unlike the philosophers Marx and Engels, with whom dialectical materialism has become synonomous, he had less success in applying his theory to the analysis of society. Nevertheless, he was a committed Republican and revolutionary. The way he differed from previous working class revolutionaries was that he totally rejected any clandestine organisation or conspiracy. First it was necessary to enlighten people with Tom Paine's principles, as developed by Carlile, and then revolution would be spontaneous and unstoppable. 'In the present state of this country,' he explained in an appendage to Joseph Brayshaw's cautionary tale of the 1820 uprising:

> **'the people have no other real duty than to make themselves acquainted with what constitutes their politcal rights... In the interim, each individual ought to prepare and hold himself ready as an armed individual, without relating to, or consulting with his neighbours, in case circumstances should ever require him to take up arms to preserve what liberty and property he may already possess against any tyrannical attempts to lessen them; or, from the force of a better knowledge and better principles, to assist in extending his liberty when the opportunity may offer.'**

In 1833, during the ferment over the failure of the Reform Act to extend the franchise to working people, Carlile encouraged his supporters through his new periodical, the *Gauntlet,* to become Republican 'volunteers' to assert their rights. Some evidently interpreted this as meaning in arms. One subscriber called himself 'A volunteer with a brace of pistols and a spear,' another 'Wants to be at them'. Two hundred and seven names, including some of women, from the Huddersfield area were printed, and not all the local lists were published. One was the son of Tom Vevers, and others were involved in the radical Political Union and, later, Chartism. Chris Tinker, who collected the signatures at his Market Walk beer shop and newsagents, sold, besides illegal unstamped papers, Republican classics such as Paine's political and theological works, Volney's *Ruin of Empires*, and Shelley's *Queen Mab*. Also, indicative of the revolutionary mood of some of his comrades and customers, he advertised *Plans for the Defence of the People* by Colonel Macerone, an illustrated manual of revolutionary street fighting, which was the 1830s and 40s equivalent of Che Guevara's *Guerilla Warfare*. Tinker, imprisoned in 1836 for selling unstamped papers, subsequently won notoriety for threatening violence against the Poor Law Commissioners and displaying fearsome looking daggers in his window.[5]

But, although Huddersfield experienced some lively election and anti-poor law riots in the 1830s, there was never again a recourse to armed uprising. Even during the attempted Chartist insurrections in Dewsbury, Sheffield and Bradford in the 1840s, no Huddersfield Radicals were implicated. Rumours of drilling were current in 1848 and a few guns were seized by the police at Almondbury, but there was no real evidence of a revolutionary conspiracy. Perhaps Carlile contributed to the decline of physical force Republicanism, as his philosophy ultimately led some Republicans into the freethought atmosphere of Socialism or mainstream Chartism. The Republican and radical reform tradition, generated in the early struggles against industrial capitalism, survived with sufficient vigour however, to provide one of the elements influencing the rebirth of Socialism in the 1890's.[6]

THE CONDESCENSION OF POSTERITY

Assessments of the risings of 1812, 1817 and 1820 were long shaped by a combination of reticent folk memory and a very limited selection of contemporary written accounts. The radical uprisings soon acquired the derisory status of a forgettable comic-opera. They became dimly recollected as the 'Folly Hall fight' and the 'April Fool's day rising', only deserving a passing mention. Luddism, by comparison, was a major tragedy which traumatised communities and, only as the scars healed, increasingly caught the literary imagination. An irreverent reference to both 1812 and 1817 was contained in a satirical radical broadside published by Joshua Hobson in 1833. *Wonderful Discovery!!* ridiculed the panic of the Yeomanry officers and magistrates who had seen the recent election riots as part of a premeditated Radical plot.

'**INTELLIGENCE has just been received by Capt. L-U-D-D A--K--N, commanding the 2nd Battalion of GREASE-HORN GUARDS, bivouacing at *Bradley Mills*, (from the SPY) that ...the enemy obtained possession last night at 6 o'Clock, of the entrenchments thrown up during the late war, by *Brigadier General CROFT,* on the left banks of the river Holm, within pistol-shot of the renowned Village of *Folly Hall*:...'**

Writing the same year, Edward Parsons in his *Miscellaneous History...* of Yorkshire towns, judged 1817 'a paltry insurrecton' not worthy of description, while 1820 was a 'mad insurrection...in which a few silly men from the dregs of the populace, without leaders, without orders, without assistance, and without arms, attempted to overturn the strongest government in the world.' When he came to write the second volume, however, he did include an outline of both events. His opinion of the Luddites was even more scathing. They were not only 'deluded' but 'diabolical' as well.

By the 1830's, the fate of the Luddites was beginning to be invoked as a cautionary tale. William Threppleton, a defector from the powerful trade union movement in Huddersfield denounced his erstwhile colleagues as dangerous revolutionaries in 1834, warning '...behold the men! The legitimate offspring of Nedd Ludd...hear their council. Is it not the same as that which under the once beguiling name of "General Ludd" caused 17 of your number to be sacrificed at York...if they are determined to have another "Lud-time'*put them in the front.'* Feargus O'Connor, the Chartist leader, in a meeting at Holmfirth in 1838, also reminded his audience of the hanged Luddites, but in the context of extolling political methods as a surer way of stopping machinery. That Luddism was alive in the popular memory was apparent that same year, when William Swaine, the chairman of the Board of Guardians, condemned opponents of the new Poor Law for law-breaking. In reply his Luddite reputation was dredged up and he was harangued about the lawfulness of 'Rawfolds fight', and slated with the epithets of 'Luddite' and 'shearbreaker', though apparently more in condemnation of his hypocrisy than in disapproval of his past.[1]

A decade later, machinery and the factory system appeared supreme. Only thirty-six years had lapsed since Luddism and in the account in his *Walks Around Huddersfield* (1848), George Searle Philips claimed to draw on the memories of the 'old man of Ashenhurst,' Apart from the interesting remark that some of those hanged were innocent, he records little detail and, while expressing sympathy with the Luddites, he thought that their struggle was doomed by progress. 'If they could have been suddenly illuminated with the knowledge of what help to man and splendour to the world lay hidden in machinery, how insane they would all have seemed, standing there with such stern thoughts ready to destroy their greatest benefactor'. One wonders what 'January Searle', who had a profound reverence for the beauties of nature, would have thought of the benefits of late twentieth century technology! Charles Hobkirk, in his *Huddersfield, its history and natural history,* (1859), also included a section on the 'Luddite Insurrection'. In the 1868 edition this was expanded to include the testimony of a 'contemporary and eyewitness' to the period, John Nowell, that it was not Horsfall, but Enoch Taylor, as the maker of the frames, 'whose life they most wished for', but he includes no other new material. He provides also an outline of the 'Folly Hall Fight' and the 1820 rising.

In 1862, when the Huddersfield publisher John Cowgill reprinted a report of the York Special Commission trials, *An Historical Account of the Luddites..,* he still saw the need to spell out the moral of his story. 'We hope that the perusal of this little book will warn all against the folly and prejudice of looking upon machinery as an evil.' By now there was sufficient social and political stability for Luddism to be regarded as a safe topic for the curious, but, although there must have been many people in their sixties and seventies with recollections of those times, there were no startling revelations. An account of local Luddism appeared in the *Huddersfield Examiner* series entitled 'Marsden Memorials' in 1864, drawing on information from people who remembered 1812, mainly 74 years old George Williams, a former employee of Horsfall, but there is no 'inside-information' about the Ludds. [2]

A full factual account was attempted in the *Huddersfield Weekly News* in 1874, which compiled information from Baines' *History of Yorkshire* and Rede's *History of York Castle,* supplemented by such official sources as the 1812 Committee of Secrecy Report and contemporary newspaper accounts, including the *Mercury* and the *Courier.* It departed from the standard moralistic condemnation of Luddism by making some efforts at analysis and relevant social comment. Analogies were drawn between Luddism and the endemic agrarian violence in Ireland - 'no secret regarding the assassination of an Irish landlord could have been better kept,' than information about the Horsfall shooting and when Walker did talk, he was 'regarded with much the same feelings of detestation as the Irish regard one of their countrymen who turn informer.' In 1878 Frank Peel's first account of Luddites, on which *Risings of the Luddites* published in 1880, was based, appeared in the *Heckmondwike Herald* of 25 Jan to 6 Aug 1878, but little of his work seems to stem from authentic local tradition. An expanded version of the *Risings*... published in 1888 did attempt to relate Luddism to the succeeding insurrections, but his language reveals his view of the participants' rebelliousness 'The more ignorant and headstrong portion of that generation never indeed seems to have wholly lost the feeling...'. Peel subscribed to the view of Luddites as stereotyped terrorists - deluded men led by the ruthless fanatic, in this case George Mellor.

The first fictional work in the Luddite genre, Charlotte Bronte's *Shirley,* appeared in 1849 and, although based on *Leeds Mercury* reports, supplemented by gleanings from the recollections of her father and other acquaintances, it reveals more about middle class attitudes than about Luddism itself. Arthur Lodge's *Sad Times - a Tale of the Luddites*, published in 1866 is not of the same literary standard and has even less historical content, being set against a very vague background of events. Some of the vagueness is intentional since the author, while clearly fascinated, is repelled by the subject, and, in the context of Horsfall's shooting, the names of H[uddersfield] and M[arsden] appear only as initial letters. In 1880 an anonymous account, interweaving fictional and actual characters and events, entitled, *Daisy Baines the Luddite's daughter*, was serialised over several months in the *Huddersfield Weekly News,* regaling its readers with , 'A Local Historical story of Thrilling Interest... There are persons still living who not only witnessed but took part in the events on which the story is founded, and the memories of the dark days still linger in many households.' This still showed some sensitivity to local feeling by thinly disguising the names of some of the participants - thus Mellor becomes 'Waller' and Horsfall, 'Horseman'. An element of local knowledge was included - a drinking song *Three Cropper Lads o' Honley,* is certainly authentic - and there was an attempt to understand the Luddites motivation, but again Mellor/Waller is very much the villain of the piece. Most of the information, as in Peel, was based on the York trials and the same documents published in the *Weekly News* in 1874.

The Luddites were definitely not compatible with the tradition of the respectable 'Lib-Lab' trade union movement of the 1890s, and Owen Balmforth, himself a former Republican, only gave them a passing mention in his *Official programme* of the *Thirty Third Trades Union Congress held in Huddersfield 1900* (p.21). 'In 1812 Huddersfield was notorious as one of the towns where the Luddites were in active resistance...' and, strangely, he refers readers, not to Peel, but to Mrs Linnaeus Bank's *'The Bond Slaves: the story of a struggle'* published in 1893. The *Bond Slaves* of the title are not the slaves of the machines or of the manufacturers but of 'the fearful oath'; and Luddites ' were never free from its obligations or its dread penalties whilst they walked the earth. The grave closed over them and their evil secrets.' The account is violently opposed to working class activity, reflecting the alarm of the middle classes at the revival of mass trade unions and socialism in the 1880s and 90s. Peel's anachronistic characterisation of the Rawfolds martyr John Booth as an Owenite, is seized upon as an opportunity to condemn all socialists. But the resurgence of the labour movement also meant that Luddism was regarded with increasing sympathy by those involved in the struggle. D. F. E. Sykes, a former Radical turned socialist, in his *History of Huddersfield and District* (Huddersfield 1910 p. 320) concluded the section on the Luddites with the observation that, 'these men were not common malefactors...though mistakenly, they laboured for their class.' His view of the Luddites was fleshed out and the sympathies of the reader aroused by a wealth of human detail in his novel *Ben o'Bills the Luddite,* which ran into several editions, and has been recently republished. Sykes knowledge was based mainly on Cowgill's 1862 *Account...* but he also drew on oral tradition. One man however, the son of Joseph Wilkinson of Lingards, who knew some of the characters around in 1812, recollected that the Luddites 'never exhibited any spite against Mr [Enoch] Taylor; he came and went where he pleased unmolested; their hatred was towards the men who bought and used the machines.' This is in direct contradiction of the 'eye-witness' account of John Nowell, recorded by Hobkirk in 1868, and with *Marsden Memorials* which claimed that the Taylors had to sleep in the fortified Woodbottom Mill for safety. It warns us how little reliance can sometimes be placed on tradition. [3]

The controversy surrounding Luddism was revived in 1929 by the Skelmanthorpe historian Fred Lawton, who recollected that, as a boy over sixty years previously he had been present with his father at the death-bed confession of a former Milnsbridge man then living in Denby Dale. 'It wor me 'at shot Horsfall' the old man supposedly said ' Mellor, Thorpe and Smith wor hanged for it. It was me 'at did it. Nah aw can dee content.' Lawton's tale was greeted with some scepticism at the time, but was he just romancing, or was there indeed someone else implicated, who escaped Radcliffe's net ?

All these accounts were based on the same corpus of original documentary sources, coloured by local anecdotes and varying degrees of artistic licence. In 1919 J. L. and B. Hammond published *The Skilled Labourer 1760-1832*, incorporating for the first time an extensive survey of Home Office records, in which Yorkshire Luddism and the rising of 1817 were placed clearly in the context of the working class response to the industrial revolution. However the Hammonds, as middle class Fabians who believed workers incapable of achieving anything without the responsible guidance of their betters, played down the revolutionary tendency in the movement, attributing conspiracies to the activities of spies and provocateurs like Oliver. This view was shared by Darvell in 1934 who concluded that the men of 1817 were 'just suckers'.

In 1963 E.P.Thompson in his *Making of the English Working Class* sought to redress the balance and rescue the Luddites and other workers from what he saw as the:

> **'enormous condescension of posterity...Their hostility to the new industrialism may have been backward looking. Their communitarian ideals may have been fantasies. Their insurrectionary conspiracies may have been foolhardy. But they lived through these times of acute social disturbance and we did not.'**

This sympathetic spirit was expressed in the *Story of Huddersfield* by Roy Brook in 1968, which described the Luddite conflict as 'industrial civil war' (p86), and George Mellor as an 'heroic figure' (p.94). The continuity with events in 1817 was also emphasised. [3]

However the condescension continues, particularly over the question of the Luddite's resort to violence. Ereira in *The Peoples' England* (1981) considered that assassination 'marked the degeneration of Luddism into banditry.' (p.114) whilst Robert Reid's *Land of Lost Content* (1988 pp.160 & 272) speaks of the Luddites' resort to assassination as Mellor 'adopting the tactics of a small time gangster' commenting that 'Mellor, potentially so attractive as a working class leader had sunk to using the methods of a thug.' These moralistic judgements betray a misunderstanding of the nature of the Luddite struggle as a form of guerrilla warfare. A small group of untrained, poorly armed and inexperienced men had taken on the might of the British government and the army. As with any guerrilla war, the weaker group must utilise any means at its disposal, and the killing of Horsfall was, in this context, a political assassination, not a common murder. Such tactics, greatly praised when committed by the French Resistance or other partisan groups against Britain's opponents, are condemned when carried out by the Luddites, or others, against the British state.

This combination of neglect, condemnation and condescension of the Luddites has on occasion been redressed by people who saw themselves as heirs to Luddism in the continuing class struggle. In 1927, a period which bears some political comparison to our own - working class defeats, the crushing of the miners and the imposition of anti-trade union legislation - a writer in the *Citizen* newspaper of the Huddersfield Labour Party looked to earlier times for inspiration,

> **'We have had our imagination stirred in Huddersfield about the Luddites by the novel written by our own local writer, D. F. E. Sykes, as well as by Charlotte Bronte's novel. Neither of these works greatly emphasise the point that the principal antipathy of the workers to the introduction of**

machinery arose out of their powerlessness to combine and regulate the conditions which followed on the new machines. The Luddite Movement takes on a new significance in the discussions of the the present Trade Union Bill. The stones of the dumb steeple cannot remain dumb. It is an excellent suggestion to take Saturday, June 18th, as a day of pilgrimage to the Dumb Steeple. It is intended to get all the surrounding constituencies to combine on that day in a great demonstration aganst the Trade Union Bill.' [4]

On 17 June the *Citizen* followed up this theme with pieces on *Shirley* and the Dumb Steeple, the latter by Ben Turner, a pioneer socialist and weavers' union leader, by now a respected national Labour movement figure. He described the Luddites as 'heroic', 'men of courage and... defenders of their families', who had had violence forced upon them.

Today, when most effective trade union action is again illegal and workers are afflicted by, 'powerlessness to combine'; when peoples' lives are still controlled by blind, inhuman economic forces and a government, representing only a powerful and wealthy elite, ruthlessly utilises the state to stamp out any attempt at resistance as in the miners' strike, the aspirations of the early Republicans, Luddites and Radicals take on a new significance. Although the monarchy has not plumbed the depths of depravity seen in the Regency period, it has lost much of its gloss and Republicanism is once more receiving serious consideration. Some of the aims of the Radicals, such as vote by ballot and universal suffrage, have been achieved, but there is still something fundamentally lacking in a parliamentary system which allows the formation of a government elected by only a minority of the population. The survival of an unelected upper chamber further emphasises that a truely democratic form of government, accountable to the people, does not yet exist.

The Luddite movement in particular has fixed itself firmly in folk history and imagination because, for many, it continues to strike a chord with their own experience, as they see the bonds of their communities destroyed by technology. Although they were by no means Socialists, the Luddites *were* fighting against the imposition of large scale industrial capitalism, which has since far surpassed their worst fears in the immensity of horrors and suffering it has unleashed on the world. George Mellor's homily, that 'a soul is more valuable than work or gold,' reveals more ethical insight than is revealed by many now hailed as great economists, politicians or philosophers.

Perhaps the only wonder is that there is little in Huddersfield and the surrounding area to commemorate those who fought for these ideals, save John Booth Close at Liversedge and a minor street at Crosland Moor named after William Horsfall - the latter hardly a fitting tribute to the aspirations of the Luddites! It is time that Huddersfield's radical history had some appropriate monument, other than that silent witness, the Dumb Steeple.

NOTES AND REFERENCES

The Rights of Man.
1.John W.Derry *Charles James Fox* (Gateshead 1972) p.293
2.Tom Paine *The Rights of Man* (Pelican edition), Paine's terminology showed that he was literally thinking mainly of the rights of *Men*, but through his association with Mary Wolstencraft, author of *Vindication of the Rights of Women* (as well as a reply to Burke, *Vindication of the Rights of Man*, published before Paine's work) he was aware of the gender bias.

Spirit of Persecution.
1.E.P.Thompson, *The Making of the English Working Class* (Pelican 1968);F.K.Donnelly and John L.Baxter 'Sheffield and the English Revolutionary Tradition 1791-1820' in Pollard and Holmes (ed) *Essays in the Economic and Social History of South Yorkshire* (Sheffield 1976) pp. 92-96; G.A.Williams *Artisans and Sanscullotes,* (London 1968)
2.Anonymous *A Serious and Candid Address to the Traders, Manufacturers and Others in Yorkshire and Lancashire* Printed by J.Brooke, Huddersfield 1793 Huddersfield Local History Library [HLHL]; Veitch,G.S, *The Genesis of Parliamentary Reform* (London 1965)
G.Williams 'True Born Britons' in *The Long March of Everyman* T.Barker (ed)(1975);Thompson p.143.
3.Stock, Percy, *Foundations* (Halifax 1933) p.488 ,490-492,This is a collection of letters relating to local Baptists.; Thompson E.P. *op.cit.* p.143.
4.Philip Ahier. ' William Whitacre and Longwood House' in *Huddersfield Daily Examiner* 5 Jan 1937 . He quotes an unpublished letter of Dyson from 1794, but according to Veitch it was 1793 when the Huddersfield petition was sent. Ahier on Beaumont in 'An Echo of the French Revolution' cutting in HLHL , unprovenanced, but apparently 1944 *Examiner.*
5.J.R.Wester 'The Volunteer Movement as an Anti-Revolutionary Force, 1793-1801, *English Historical Review,* October 1956.
6.*Foundations* p.151

Tyrants Tremble.
1.*Leeds Mercury (LM)* 1 Feb 1800; Quarter Session Bundles 1800, West Yorkshire records Office, Wakefield (these refer to the defendant as Hannah Bray). Radcliffe MSS 578. 1 (Rad.MSS) (papers deposited in Leeds City Archives (LCA) by the late Sir Everard Radcliffe of Rudding Park.
2.Public Records Office, Home Office papers (HO) Coke to Portland 24 Mar 1801 (quoted in A.D.Harvey *Britain in the Early 19th Century:(* 1978); House of Lords Committee of Secrecy 1801.; compare Rev.Hay's letter to Portland 15 Jan 1801, about oath administered in Saddleworth with Ezekiel quote in preface. Copy in, Wentworth Woodhouse Muniments, Fitzwilliam papers, (F), Sheffield City Libraries. , F.45/43-39.
3.John Crowder, Huddersfield, (another letter refers to him collecting rents for Ramsden) to B.Cooke at Westminster 31 March 1801. F 45/9,11,12,18,20,21
4. Rad. MSS 1.578.
5.This account is based on 'Jacobinism and Unrest in the Huddersfield Area 1799-1803' in *Old West Riding* Vol.2 No.1. Spring 1982; For the national background see Roger Wells *Insurrection - The British Experience 1795-1803* (Gloucester 1983);Rad MSS 1; HO.42/65.; Fletcher to HO 3 Apr 1802; F.45/51.Another prospective spy,Fred Flower wrote to the Home Office in 1802 offering his services ,having demonstrated his loyalty by the fact that 'once in Huddersfield at the moment of a riot breaking out in the principle street, stopped it a great risk by taking a football from one of the mob which was thrown down as a signal of their diabolical intentions...'.
6.HO 42/62.404.Fitzwilliam at Hull to HO 16 Aug 1801. J.Coke, Wakefield to HO 19 Aug Grange Moor meeting last Saturday week, 1800 present. F.45/18. Radcliffe to Fitzwilliam 23 May 1801.In commmunication with Hay who has dispersed meetings.F.45/20 Dawson, Wakefield to Portland 27 Jul 1801. He thought 'Nocturnal meetings very frequent indeed'
7. F.45/64 Radcliffe to Fitzwilliam, 24 July 1802 the enclosed constitution and card are in F.45/71-1,71-3.
8. F.45/65.
9. F.45/82; F.45/88, Bernard to Fitzwilliam 6 Sep 1802. Bernard thought the threatening letter had been written by some one who could 'spell and write much better' than they pretended.

10. F.45/94;. Henry Legge to Fitzwilliam 20 Sep. 1802. Rad. MS 1.578, it is not clear whether the copy of the Constitution Legge reported was seized by Radcliffe. F.45/95 Pelham to Fitzwilliam; Edward Harling also gave information on Almondbury Republicans with whom he appeared familiar. He was, at this time, a bankrupt *LM* 3 Oct 1801, *LM* 29 May 1802.

11. Fitzwilliam 45/9.May to Leeds to Mary Tucker;F.45/83. Cookson, Leeds mayor, to Fitzwilliam 30 Aug 1802, about strike.; *Parliamentary Papers* 1806, Select 'Committee on the State of the Woollen Manufacture 1806', James Fletcher's evidence; for background to Croppers Institution see A.J.Brooke, 'Trade Unions and Labour Disputes' in *Huddersfield - A Most Handsome Town* Hilary Haigh (Ed) (Huddersfield 1992.) for W.Country connexion see Kenneth Ponting, *The Woollen Industry of South West England* (Bath 1971); A.Randall *Before the Luddites* (Cambridge 1991).

12.*LM* 9 Apr 1803;Rad MSS1 578; F.45/108,118,119; *LM* 25 Sep 1802, *LM* 22 Jan 1803; *LM* 20 Aug 1803.

13. PP.1806. p.321; *LM* 19 Jul 1806.

14. *LM* 21 May 1808.

15.*LM* 8 Dec 1807; *LM* 20 Feb 1808; *LM* 5 Mar 1808.

16. *LM* 5 Jun 1809;*Remarks on an Advertisement which appeared in the Leeds Intelligencer of July 17 1809 Signed R.H.Beaumont, Magistrate, in Two Letters to the Author.* R.Hurst printer, Wakefield 1809, also *LM* 22 Jul 1809.

17.*LM* 4 Jun 1808, croppers meeting; W.B.Crump, *The Leeds Woollen Industry* (Leeds 1931) pp.229-230, 'Clerk to General Ludd' to Mr Smith, Hillend.

Metropolis of Discontent

1. For accounts of Huddersfield Luddism see Frank Peel *The Rising of Luddites etc* (Heckmondwike 1888), which has influenced most subsequent accounts. Also E.P.Thompson, op. cit., J.&.B.Hammond *The Skilled Labourer 1760-1832* (London 1919); F.Darvall, *Popular Disturbances and Public Order in Regency England* (London 1969); M.I.Thomis *The Luddites ;* M.I.Thomis & P.Holt *Threats of Revolution in Britain 1789-1848* (Macmillan 1977); for an accurate and clear outline of Luddism which relates events to local topography, Lesley Kipling & Nick Hall, *On the Trail of the Luddites* (Hebden bridge 1982). The most recent account, which, while detailed and very readable, fails to put Luddism in its full local or national political and social context, is in Robert Reid *Land of Lost Content - The Luddite revolt.1812* (London 1986). The 'Metropolis of Discontent' description is from Hansard *Proceedings of the Special Commission at York* (1813). (SCY)

2. Treasury Solicitor's brief TS11/812. 2670 on William Hill's deposition, describes the first attack.

3.HO.40.1/7(3).

4.HO.40.1/1 (174-283). Depositions. John Swallow.

5. HO.42/121. Radcliffe to Home Office 17 Mar: Enclosure.

6.TS11/812.2666, William Hall, Joseph Drake depositions. Those identified as taken part in the attack on Vickerman's included George Mellor, with his scythe-blade sword: William Thorpe; Tom Smith carrying a hatchet; Jonathan Dean a hammerman; James Brook wearing a large cocked hat and wielding a hatchet; his brother George Brook; John Brook armed with a pistol; Sam Booth carrying a blunderbus; James Varley, Mark Hill, Charles Thornton, Joshua Schofield and Joseph Thornton.

7.*LM* 11 April 1812; *LM* 14 Aug 1813 Rad 126/32.

8.Rad MS 126/46 1 May 1812.

9.Rad MS 126/27

10.HO.40/1.50 Letter to Smith of Hillend, Crump, *Leeds Woollen Industry* pp229-230; Rad MS 126/26 Radcliffe to HO 17 Mar 1812.

11.*LM* 25 Apr 1812;HO.40/1.1; Rad MS 3797/68, Walker's deposition given at Chester, 8 Nov.; Rad MS 126/38.

12.HO.42/123, examination of C.Dyson 3 April.; TS11/812.2670; *LM* 11 Jul 1812; HO.42/125; *LM* 6 Jun, 18 Jul 1812.

13.*LM* 20 Jun 1812;York S.C. trial of Swallow et.al.;*LM* 11 Jul 1812;York S.C.trial of Joseph Brook.

14. F.46/70, Richard Walker 18 Jul.; F.46/71, depositions on Clifton attack.

15.*LM* 20 Jun 1812; Rad MS 3797/97, Radcliffe to Lascelles, 25 Jan 1813; TS.2666. Constable Blythe appears to have been a truculent character. He disappeared in 1835 walking home from Honley after refusing to pay someone for looking after his run-away horse. His hat was found in the river Holme.

16. Francis Raynes *An Appeal to the People...'* (London 1817); York Special Commission Proceedings (YSC); Rad MS 3797/78, contains the oath appended to a Cotton Weavers' Address not only calling for a union of trades but also political action.

17.HO.42.125.Barrowclough's deposition; Rad MS 3797/6 Hay to Radcliffe 10 Jul 1812 expresses doubts on Barrowclough's evidence - and sanity. Joseph died less than three years later and, intestate. His brother William, also a carpentar, acted as assignee, *LM* 11 Nov. 1815. A George Weightman, a sawyer of Pentrich in Derbyshire, was prominent in 1817, and may have visited the area then. PRO.HO.40/2 (118) John Knight at Dobcross to General Acland at Huddersfield 19 Sep 1812; HO.42/127; W.P.Acland to Raynes 22 Sep. 1812, in Raynes *op.cit.* p.114-115;.HO.42/127 Lloyd to Beckett, 20 Sep; Rad MS 3797/71,'delegates orders'; Rad MS 126/82 and 83, 27 Jun, Cross Pipes meetings.

18. Rad.126/72, Radcliffe to Ryder 16 May; Rad. 1.578, Radcliffe to Pickford 12 May 1812;*LM* 25 Apr, F.45/130, 133, Carlton attack; *LM* 16 May, Dewsbury; F.46/51 Maitland to F. 20 Aug, Rastrick.

19.SCY Haigh's trial; Patrick Doring's trial TS.2666, *LM* 1 Aug 1816; Rad MS 126/113 31 Dec 1812.

20. Hammonds op. cit. p. 308; Rad.3797/66 Lloyd's 'observations relative to the prisoners in York...'; Secret Committee Report, published in *HWN* 1874

21.HO.42/129 John Bates examination; *LM* 2 May 1812, woman stoned; HO 42/122; Rad 126/93 Radcliffe to Fitzwilliam 27 Oct;HO 42/90.; Rad 126/90.; Rad MS 3797/45 Acland to Radcliffe 1 Oct, Lockwood incident.; Rad MS 3797/43 Lt. Cooper to Radcliffe 29 Sep; 3797/41 Radcliffe to Sidmouth 28 Sep 1812; Raynes to Acland 7 Nov, quoted in Reid, *op.cit.* p.225.

22. *LM* 25 Apr 1812; Peel p. 91; Thompson op. cit.p 615; Hammonds pp.114-116.

23. *LM* 18 Apr 1812; *Political Register* 18 Apr 1812, reprinted in *HWN* Jun 1874; R.126/32; For a moving account of the arrival of the cortege in Huddersfield, supposedly drawn from popular tradition, see 'Daisy Baines', Chapter LIV, *Huddersfield Weekly News* 2 Apr 1881.

24.*HWN* 1874, quoting from Rede's *History of York Castle.*

25.TS.2666.Brief of case against Doring; *LM* 1 August 1812, Doring's trial; *LM* 3 Apr 1816, 'Hue and Cry', *LM* 21 Sep 1816, committed to York; *LM* 19 Apr 1817, hanged.

26.HO.42/146. Robert Say, Captain of the Norfolk Militia at Holmfirth to Gen. Acland;*LM* 20 Jul 1811, three other Huddersfield croppers were also gaoled then as debtors , perhaps an indication of the parlous state of the trade; Rad. 3797/73, Thos Selby, deposition; 3797/95, Radcliffe to Hobhouse 16 Jan 1813.

27. Rad.126/135, William Hobson's deposition, 126/133 John, Joseph and Sarah Drake's depositions. A Joseph Drake, working for the cloth dresser John Drake, was involved in the Rawfold attack.

28. *LM* 11 April 1812;*LM* 16 May 1812.

29. Rad.3797/3. Lloyd to Radcliffe 2 July 1812; HO.40/2/2.159;HO.40/2/3.20 Vickerman, Taylor Hill to Acland 28 Aug 1812.

30.*Huddersfield Examiner (Weekly) (HEW)* 30 Sep 1871 Williams obituary.

31. Rad.3797/73, Affidavit against Harling; Rad.126/91; /95; Rad.3797/ 99 Radcliffe to Beckett, 5 Jun 1813..

32. WYAS KC.DD/AH 47, (this refers to transcripts from the HO record made by Philip Ahier)- Ahier MS 12 Oct ; Rad.3797/33. Acland to Radcliffe 13 Sep; /53 Captain Thornton 14 Oct; /35 Raynes complaint against Horrocks 13 Sep and /47 Hammond Roberson, dispute settled 5 Oct 1812; Acland detected strong rivalry between the Specials, Radcliffe and the military. 3797/44 Acland to Radcliffe 13 Sep. 1812.

33. Milnes *Warning Voice* p.172; Rad. 126/75. Gamaliel Lloyd to Radcliffe.

34. One senior officer, Major Richard Bullen, had a daughter Jemima baptised on 3 Feb 1813; *LM* 29 Aug 1812; Calderdale Archives KMA 1552/2, Littlewood, Huddersfield to Commissioners of Barracks Dept, London 27 Feb 1816. ; Sykes *History of Huddersfield &c....* (Worker Press) p. 305 (quoting W. Thornbury *Old Stories Retold*) describes the troops "impoverishing and sometimes ruining the landlords, irritating the high-spirited, oppressing the neutral, and contaminating the whole neighbourhood" Rad.3797/2, rental of several alarm posts1 Jul , /27, 26 Aug. list of guard posts; .HE 9 Jan 1864 *Marsden Memorials*; Mary Jagger *History of Honley.* mentions a 10 o'clock curfew.

35. *LM* 9 May 1812; KMA 1552/1, Memorandum, Huddersfield adjourned sessions, 7 Aug 1812, KMA 1552/2 list of arms. (Thanks to John Rumsby for these references); Philip Ahier, 'Not Remnant of a Fort' *Huddersfield Examiner* (*HE*) 11 May 1938.

36. *LM* 25 Apr; WWM.F.46/34;39; *LM* 9 May 1812.

37. Rad. 37397/33 Acland to Radcliffe, 13 September; Ahier MS..

38. HO. 42/129, Fitzwilliam to HO, 4 Nov; Byron's speech is reprinted in *HWN* 13 Jun 1874 ; the description of the penal code is from the account by Tory MP and barrister Ian Gilmour, *Riot, Risings and Revolution - Governance and violence in 18th century England*' (London 1992) p.163.

39. Woodbottom Mill description in 'Marsden Memorials' *HE* 23 Jan 1864; Rad 126/114.

40. Rad.126/72 Lloyd; /92 Fitzwilliam 26 Oct; /94 29 Oct.

41. F.46/53 Maitland 6 Sep q. Reid p.210; HO. 42 /127 q. Hammonds p.321.Rad.126/93 Radcliffe 27 Oct.

42. F.46/91 Maitland to Fitzwilliam 3 Nov 1812; HO.42/129 4 Nov. Maitland to Sidmouth q. Reid p.223.; HO. 42.132, 7 Jan. q. Hammonds p.324

43. HO.42.134 17 Jun 1813.

44. HO.42.127 Maitland 13 Sep. q. Hammonds p.321.

45. HO.42/128 1 Oct q. Hammonds p. 322; Rad.126/96;Ahier MS, Acland 18 Oct.; HO.42/123 q.Reid p.235.

46 Rede q. *HWN* 5 Sep 1874, Reid op. cit. p. 231; Ahier MS 26 Dec.

b.Rad.126/118; 126/120. Radcliffe to Fitzwilliam.126/125 Fitzwilliam to Radcliffe 25 Jan 1813;126/118 Hobhouse to Radcliffe 22 Jan 1813.

48. Rad.MS.3797/66, Lloyd's observation on prisoners at York; Rad.3797/57, Radcliffe to Milne 19 Oct. 1812, Richard Tattersall; Rad MS 3797/48 from War Office to Sidmouth, Joshua Haigh. 3797/50 Norton at York to Radcliffe, Joshua Haigh probably innocent; Ahier MS HO Acland to Maitland 24 Sep; HO.42/125 Barrowclough's deposition; 3797/20 Radcliffe to Sidmouth 18 Aug 1812 Barrowclough's evidence against Samuel Haigh. HO.42/128, Lloyd to Becket 8 Oct, re. 'woman Walker' ev. against Joshua Haigh. If the Joshua who was involved at Rawfolds was the deserter, it is not clear whether he enlisted before the attack or afterwards to avoid arrest. Evidence that the 51st regiment was recruiting locally appears in the case of Fred Thornton of Rastrick. He was fined £20 by Radcliffe, for giving his hat to help Joseph Morton disguise himself when deserting on Christmas Eve, 1813, apparently from a recruiting party at the Clothiers Arms. *LM* 8 Jan 1814.

49. Ahier HO. MS.Acland 18 Oct; HO. 42.2/5 suspects, q.Reid p.209; HO.42/129 11 Oct. q.Reid pp.215-216.

50. Rad.3797/58 Walker to Radcliffe 22 Oct 1812.

51. TS.2670; Rad.126/127. HO. 40 2/3. Cartwright to Acland 30 Jan 1813, q Reid p.268;

 Ahier *Legends of Huddersfield* p.27.

52. Lloyd and Mrs Walker q. Hammonds p.323. Reid *op. cit.* p.217;

Ahier MS HO to Acland 20 Oct, 21 Oct,22 Oct. 1812; LM 31 Oct.

53. Joseph Wood, small notebook. no. 51 in *Plain Country Friends* p.101. from private collections loaned to the authors for their research, Joseph Wood collection, small notebooks 1-63.

54. HO.40/2/2.159 ; Reid p. 213 interprets the 'V' letter, which he describes as in 'an educated hand' as coming from a Varley, who had a nephew apprenticed to Joseph Mellor. But there was no apprentice of this name at Mellors', whereas Vickerman's nephew undoubtedly did work there.

55. WYAS.KC.312, Nowell papers, 13/6 *Early scientific friends* MS; 13/15 Letter Hobkirk to Nowell 13 November 1867.

Death or Liberty

1. Rad.126/ 117 22 Jan, re; Cartwright meeting; /123, 27 Jan 1813, Lascelles to Radcliffe. Sam Clay was involved in an assault case when he was accused of being a 'Luddite' because of his support for reform, WYAS, KC165/80. Struggling with a failing business and supporting a large family he died aged 53 in 1833 after falling over a cart shaft. *Halifax Guardian* 16 Feb 1833,

2. *LM* 24 Jul 1813.

3. Rad.3797/95 Beckett to Radcliffe 24 May 1813 ; /98;/99; /100 for Brook. This may be the same John Drake who informed against Tom Riley. The government refused to back Radcliffe in prosecuting Brook; *LM* 4 Jun 1814; Rad 126/132;126/136; HO.42/148, Allison to HO 26 Feb. 1816 (q. Darvell p.155) says it was on the 24 Feb (the fourth anniversary of the first 1812 attack !) ; Mayall's date of 3 Mar, in*Annals of Yorkshire* must be wrong; Rad.1.578, Frances Pickford (Radcliffe's daughter) to Radcliffe 18 Mar 1816 rejoicing to hear that troops have arrived; Calderdale Archives KMA 1552/2, Littlewood, Huddersfield to Commissioners of Barracks Dept, London 27 Feb 1816; thanks to John Rumsby for this reference; 'Huddersfield 70 years ago', first Irish residents in *HEW* 8 Jun 1878

4. Rad.1.578, John Carr, Leeds to Radcliffe 19 Nov 1816; HO.42/166. Richard Lee's deposition.

5. *LM* 18 Jan 1817; *LI* 20 Jan 1817,It is not clear whether the site of the meeting was Rashcliffe or Almondbury Bank.

6. Samuel Bamford, *Passages in the Life of a Radical* (Oxford UP 1984) Chapters 4-7 passim; H.W.C. Davis, 'Lancashire Reformers 1816-1817' *Bull. of John Rylands Library* 1925, pp.47-79 particularly 70-71.

7.*LM* 25 Jan 1817

8.HO.42/161 Edward Tyker of Thornhill Edge to HO, 3 March 1817.

9.*LI* 17 Feb 1817;*LM* 15 Feb 1817; *LM* 1 Mar 1817.

10. Davis *op. cit.* 58-59; Bamford *op.cit.*29-36, 64-69.*LM* 14 Feb 1818, John Lancaster [sic] petition .

11.HO.42/165. Huddersfield magistrates to HO, 9 May; *LM* 5 Apr 1817;*LM* 12 Apr 1817.

12. This account of the preparation of the uprising is compiled from F.186.Armytage to Fitzwilliam 12 June 1817; 188.Deposition of William Schofield of Honley; 189-1.Deposition of John Buckley of Longroyd Bridge; 190. John Langley of Deanhouse; 191.Tom Riley deposition.; 193.Matthew Riley deposition; HO.42/165. Tom Bradley, deposition; HO.42/166, brief against Smaller; HO.42/166 Brief against Johnson, Thewlis et.al. for stealing arms in Honley HO.40/9.(4).500 Brief re. Ben Whiteley, Riley, Hepponstall and Richard Lee, especially deposition of latter taken before B.H.Allen.

13. Mitchell's account of his arrest and imprisonment is given in his petition for release presented to the House of Commons 13 Feb.1818.

14.HO.40/9(2) 17-24 Oliver's own account of his activities;*LM* 21 Jun;19 Jul 1817.; For Tom Bacon and the Derbyshire uprising see the highly readable, but mis-titled, *England's Last Revolution - Pentrich 1817* by John Stevens (Buxton 1977).

15.HO. 42/165;R. Lee, deposition mentions Beaumont and the Lockwood man at Thurlestone meeting.

16.HO 42/165 Bradley's depos; 42/166;WWM f.45/189 Buckley's deposition.

17.*LM* 14 Jun;21 Jun 1817

18.*LM* 2 Aug 1817, account of trial, Hannah Dyson, Samuel Wimpenny, J.Kemp, Susan Hirst, J.Robinson, George Holron, Richard Littlewood, George Boothroyd, evidence.

19.*LM* 2 Aug, 9 Aug 1817, account of trial. George Armitage, Nathan Taylor, Captain John Armitage, David Alexander, George Whitehead, according to Whitehead there were about 400 insurgents but David Alexander estimated only 60 to 70 on the bridge. Even if there were others in the fields, dozens rather than hundreds appear more probable.

20. Stevens. *op. cit.*

21.*LM* 14 Jun - 15 Jul 1817, passim; F.45/185 Armitage to Fitzwilliam 9 June.186 12 Jun 1817.

22.*LI* 16 Jun-23 Jul 1817; *LM* 27 Feb 1818.

23.TS.11.4134. John Littlewood's bill for searching for George Taylor at Manchester, Stockport and other places £5.12s.6d.; House of Commons 23 Feb. Lee's petition; *Ibid.* 24 Feb Whiteley's petition also in *LM* 4 and 25 Apr 1818, and 9 May for their cases.

Those arrested were, according to *Mercury* reports;

Arms stealing.

Jonathan Bailey	(25) clothier,	Pog Ing.
Jonathan Brook	(28) Clothdresser,	Meltham.
Ben Donkersley,	(29) weaver,	Honley
Isaac Johnson,	(33) labourer,	Holmfirth.
Abraham Oldham,	(22) labourer,	Marsh Platt.
John Oldham,	(20) labourer,	Marsh Platt.
Joseph Sykes,	(41) clothier,	Honley.
Joshua Thewles,	(24) labourer,	Holmfirth.
Ben Taylor,	(24) fancy weaver,	Honley.
John Kinder,	(41) Clothdresser,	Honley.

24.*LM* 2 Aug, 9 Aug 1817, account of trial George Armitage, Nathan Taylor, Captain John Armitage, David Alexander, George Whitehead, William Stanley, shoemaker, James Drake, cloth dresser, John Blaydes, tailor, James Woodhouse. Eli Dyson, John Thornton, William Milnes evidence.

25.*LM* 13 Dec 1817, release of Lee and Whiteley; House of Commons , petition of Lee 23 Feb 1818; Whiteley 24 Feb 1818; *LM* 4 April, 25 Apr 1818, letters from Lee; *LM* 9 May 1818, letters from Whiteley and Lee; *LI* 9 Mar 1818 attack on accounts of Riley, Lee and Whiteley.

Notes and References

Tumultously Assembling.

Ben Brook,	(18) weaver,	Salford.
Joseph Beaumont,	(23) Clothdresser,	Lockwood.
William Crowther	(17) shoemaker.	Lockwood.
Ben Green	(22) Clothdresser,	Honley.
Joseph Haigh,	(20) weaver,	Berry Brow.
Joseph Jysop,	(21) Clothdresser,	Lockwood.
Ben Lockwood,	(19) Clothdresser,	Salford.
James Oldham,	(25) Clothdresser,	Berry Brow.
John Oldfield,	(31) weaver,	Magbridge
Abraham Oldfield	(31) weaver.	Steps.
George Woffenden	(22) Clothdresser,	Lockwood.
John Wilson,	(19) Clothdresser,	Lockwood.

LM 14 Jun; 21 Jun; 25 Jul 1817

The Goddess of Freedom.

1.*LM* 14 Feb 1818; *ibid.*, case of John Lancaster of Almondbury; *LM* 28 Mar 1818, Whiteley's letter; *LM* 18 Apr.25 Apr 1818, Lee's experiences in York; *LM* 28 Feb 1818, case of Tom Riley, *LM* 27 Feb 1819, letter from R.Riley, Halifax.

2.*LM* July passim; *LM* 10 Oct,7 Nov 1818 Barnsley weavers' strike meetings and arrests;*LM* 20 Feb 1819, St Helens;*LM* 4 Dec 1819, Low Moor and Bowling colliers wages; *LM* 29 May,5 Jun 1819 Carlisle weavers;*LM* 24 Apr;12 Jun 1819 Leeds unemployed: *LM* 6 Mar 1819, letter re. croppers from 'Cosmopolitan' suggesting emigration for croppers; *LM* 20 Mar 1819, letter 'Benevolus' reduction in employment of croppers and return of soldiers.' et.seq.

3.*LM* 14 Nov 1818 'Pardon Asked'; *LM* 3 Jul 1819, Dewsbury Weavers Union; *LM* 15 Jan 1820, two Heckmondwike blanket weavers committed to York for illegal combination;*LM* 25 Dec 1819, John Robinson and John Goodair, committed to York for enticing colliers to enter unlawful combination.*LM* 26 Feb 1820, 10 blanket weavers arrested for riot and assault.

4.*LM* 3 Jul 1819;*LM* 24 Jul 1819.

5.*LM* 12 Jun 1819.

6.TS.11/1013, Jos. Tyas, deposition, HO.40/12. Joseph Hirst, deposition;WWM.F46/127, Tempest Tiffany appears in a list of those taking the oath of alliegiance before a Halifax magistrate in 1813. So does the name Joseph Starkey, involved with Tiffany in the 1820 rising.

7. *LM.* 7 Aug 1819. The verse is from *The Cotter's Saturday Night.* HO 42/191. Captain Sibthorpe to Byng 3 August.

8.For Peterloo see Bamford, *op. cit*; Joyce Marlowe, *The Peterloo Massacre* (1969); *LM* 21 Aug 1819.

9.*LM* 4 Sep 1819

10.*LM* 30 Oct 1819.11.*LM* 13 Nov 1819.

Reformers Stand True

1.For the wider background to the 1820 uprising, and particularly the role of the Barnsley Radicals see F.K.Donnelly's Ph.D thesis 'The General Rising 1820' (Sheffield University 1975); John Baxter 'Origins of the Social War...in South Yorkshire 1750-1850 Sheffield PhD 1976, a copy of which is in Barnsley Local History Library.; Also F.J.Kaijage 'Working Class Radicalism in Barnsley' in*Essays in the Economic and Social History of South Yorkshire.* S.Pollard and C.Holmes (eds) (Sheffield 1976) 118-134.

HO.42/161 Fletcher at Bolton to Hobhouse at HO.

2. 'Statement of Joseph Brayshaw, relating to his political mission, and the persons who instigated him to make it.' *Republican* Vol. VI No. 19 4 Oct 1822 p.582 to 590.; The dates Brayshaw's departure and return to Leeds are not mentioned, though it must have been before Thistlewood's arrest on 23 February. For Arthur Thistlewood and the preparations in London see David Johnson *Regency Revolution* (Salisbury 1974).; B.H.Allen to Hobhouse 28 Feb 1820.; For Scotland see Thomis & Holt, *op.cit.*.Ch.3 passim , this also refers to Brayshaw not only being in the Glasgow area at the end of March but also helping to draw up a revolutionary proclamation announcing the establishment of a Provisional Government on 1 April - and

staying at the house of James Wilson, executed for his part in the uprising. If this is the case he had clearly not simply played a passive role as observer of the preparations, or disassociated himself from the uprising.: HO.40/2.13.120 B.Haigh Allen to Hobhouse 8 May 1820 on Pilling.

3._LM_ 29 Jan 1820.;HO.40/12.67 John Allison at Huddersfield to Hobhouse 5 April 1820.

4.HO.40/11 letter to Byng 25 Feb 1820; HO.40/11.207 letter to Hobhouse, 14 mar 1820._LM_ 15 Apr 1820 - the _Mercury_ refused to publish a letter from Healey thanking the 'Friends of Reform' in Leeds, Halifax, Bradford and Huddersfield since they thought it might implicate him (and the paper) with the insurrection.; Bamford, _op.cit._p.267

5.TS.11/1013, TS.11/4132 Samuel Norcliffe's deposition and brief.

6.TS.11.1013 George Barker, deposition;TS.11/4132, Joseph Barker, deposition.

7._LI_ 3 Apr 1820;_LM_ 8 Apr 1820;HO.40/12.16a. deposition of Whitehead and Gill, 30 March.

8. HO.42/12 Joshua Hirst's deposition.;_LM_ 9 Apr 1820

9.TS.11/4132, Halstead; HO.40/12 (50) Mitchell; TS.11/1013, Tiffany.

10._LM_ 10 Apr 1820.

11.TS.11/1013. Morgan's deposition.

12._LM_ 15 Apr,22 Apr 1820; LI 17 Apr 1820; _Manchester Observer_ 15 Apr 1820; HO.40/16 Tom Ferrimond's examination; TS.11/1013. Tom Morgan's deposition.Donnelly _op. cit._ Kaijage, _op. cit._ If Comstive and Addy were the mounted men who reportedly led the rebels then this could account for their disappearance. For list of Barnsley rebels see Baxter thesis.

13.HO.40.11/12,TS.11/1013; I have corrected most of the original spelling and grammer for ease of reading, it is quoted in Thompson op. cit. p.777 with original orthography.

14._LM_ 22 Apr, 29 Apr 1820; HO.40/12 ii George Palmer's examination.HO.40/2.13 (12) B.H.Allen to Hobhouse 8 May; (149) Allen to Hobhouse,11 May; (228) Allen to Hobhouse 3 Jun 1820.

15._LM_ 15 Apr,22 Apr, 13 May, 20 May, 27 May 1820.

16._LM_ 5 Oct 1822.

17. HO. 40/16 Allen to Byng 4 Jan 1821; Byng to HO 6 Jan.

May Revolutions Never Cease

1. _Republican_ vol.IV no. 16 15 Dec 1820.

2.Marsden Memorials in _HE_ 6 Jun 1863; John Nowell, reminiscences, transcription 'Taylors of Marsden, my Early Scientific Friends' in Huddersfield Local History Library..

3._Republican_ Vol.V.25 Jan 1822 pp 108-110;vi 4 Oct 1822 pp. 595-597;vii. No.7 14 Feb 1823 pp. 211-213. April 1824. pp. 554 [sic]-455. Robert Taylor worked as a child at Haigh's cotton factory, and Ottiwells Mill in Marsden until 1809, when he joined Taylor's foundry and became a proficient mechanic and steam engine expert .His obituary described him as 'self cultured', _HE_ 11 Jan 1868

4._Republican_ vii. 28 Feb 1823; January 1824 pp. 181-184.Royle _Victorian Infidels,_

5. _Gauntlet_ 31 Mar, 5 May, 16 Jul, 8 Sep. 1833.

6.For a brief outline of later local republicanism see A. Brooke_Hall of Science-Socialism and Co-operation in Huddersfield c.1830-1848._(Huddersfield 1993).

Condescension of Posterity

1. _LM_ 24 May 1834;_NS_ 10 Nov. 1838 ;_HG_ 13 Feb 1838.

2 _An Historical Account of the Luddites...,._ (Huddersfield 1862); _HEW_ 30 Sep 1871 Williams obituary.

3. For the argument that Luddism was not revolutionary and had no relation to the revolutionary movements which suceeded it see, H. A. Hargreaves 'The Metropolis of Discontent' in_Huddersfield -A Most Handsome Town,_ Hilary Haigh (Ed) (Huddersfield 1992.)

4._The Citizen_ 20 May 1927.

INDEX

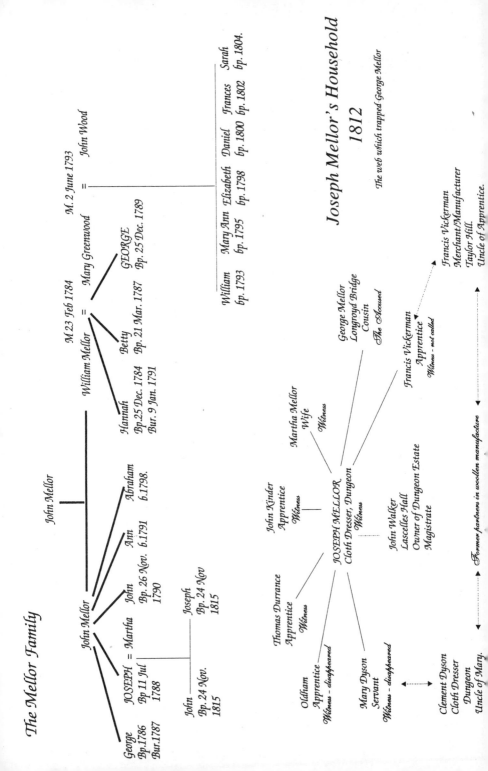

The Mellor Family

John Mellor

John Mellor ——————— William Mellor   M 23 Feb 1784   = Mary Greenwood   M. 2 June 1793   = John Wood

Children of John Mellor:

George
Bp.1786
Bur.1787

JOSEPH = Martha
Bp 11 Jul
1788

John
Bp. 26 Nov.
1790

Ann
b.1791

Abraham
b.1798.

John
Bp. 24 Nov.
1815

Joseph
Bp.24 Nov
1815

Children of William Mellor & Mary Greenwood:

Hannah
Bp.25 Dec. 1784
Bur. 9 Jan. 1791

Betty
Bp. 21 Mar. 1787

GEORGE
Bp. 25 Dec. 1789

Children of Mary Greenwood & John Wood:

William
bp. 1793

Mary Ann
bp. 1795

Elizabeth
bp. 1798

Daniel
bp. 1800

Frances
bp. 1802

Sarah
bp. 1804.

Joseph Mellor's Household
1812

The web which trapped George Mellor

JOSEPH MELLOR,
Cloth Dresser, Dungeon

Martha Mellor
Wife
Witness

John Kinder
Apprentice
Witness

Thomas Durrance
Apprentice
Witness

Oldham
Apprentice
Witness - disappeared

Mary Dyson
Servant
Witness - disappeared

Clement Dyson
Cloth Dresser
Dungeon
Uncle of Mary.

George Mellor
Longroyd Bridge
Cousin
The Accused

Francis Vickerman
Apprentice
Witness - not called

John Walker
Lascelles Hall
Owner of Dungeon Estate
Magistrate

Francis Vickerman
Merchant/Manufacturer
Taylor Hill.
Uncle of Apprentice.

◄——————— *Former partners in woollen manufacture* ——————►